ALAN TOMS

What Have We To Give? Bible Devotions from a Missionary to Burma – Volume 2

HAYES PRESS Christian Publisher

Abbreviations of Bible versions are as follows:

RV – Revised Version (1881–5)

RVM – Revised Version Margin

RSV – Revised Standard Version (1946–52)

RSVM – Revised Standard Version Margin

NIV – New International Version (English 1979)

NKJV – New King James Version (1982)

NKJVM – New King James Version Margin

From the beginning, Alan Toms predominately quoted and cited the RV, citing the RSV for the most part only in 1984, and the NKJV mainly from 2000 – 2001 onwards. He used other versions more sparingly. In the main, this use of RV and NKJV is clear enough to be unlabelled in this text. Nevertheless, the familiar labels (above) are used where it is necessary to avoid possible ambiguity.

Second edition

This book was professionally typeset on Reedsy.
Find out more at reedsy.com

Contents

Acknowledgement

Hayes Press made available the main body of Alan Toms' original writings in Needed Truth for this publication. K.J. Smith (Victoria) converted these to a standard printed format. The published excerpts were chosen primarily by A.C. Bishop and A.M. Hope (Musselburgh) and compiled by R.H. Fisher (Bathgate) prior to their final editing by M.S. Elliott (Crowborough), J.T. Needham (Birmingham) and I.E. Penn (Nottingham), who also wrote the Introduction with help from Mrs Gill Toms (Canada).

SIXTY SIX: EPAPHRAS

Epaphras was a Colossian. He's mentioned only three times in the Scriptures, but Paul says so much about him in those three references that we feel we know him well. He describes him as a faithful minister of Christ. That's what he was to the Christians in Colossae. He was their teacher. He put God's word into their hearts, and there it bore fruit and increased. 'Make disciples' the Lord Jesus said, before He went back to heaven, 'baptizing them … teaching them to observe all things whatsoever I commanded you', and that's what Epaphras did. He showed them Christ in the Scriptures, so appealingly that they wanted to follow Him too. And when they started to follow he was at hand to encourage them, until they gathered strength themselves and were able to go out and help others.

But Epaphras wasn't always at Colossae. Something happened that he found himself in prison at Rome, along with the apostle Paul. What it was, we're not told. So his teaching work among the Colossians was over. But he could still reach them through prayer. And that's what he did. This dear man gave himself to a new ministry on behalf of those Christians who were now so far away and yet so close to his heart. He gave himself to prayer. He literally gave himself to it. The language Paul uses to describe his praying is most arresting. He's always striving for you in his prayers, he wrote. It's the word used of an athlete in the games. It means to agonize. See the runner pounding down the course, every muscle strained; only one object in view - to reach the goal. That's the sort of energy and concentration Epaphras brought into his praying. Not just a few minutes by his bedside morning and evening. No! This was his work. 'I bear him witness' said the apostle, 'that he hath much labour for you, and for them in Laodicea, and for them in Hierapolis' (Colossians 4:13).

So his concern reached beyond the Christians in his home church, to those in neighbouring churches. What a man he was!

SIXTY-SEVEN: PRISCILLA AND AQUILA

The apostle Peter uses a lovely expression of a Christian husband and wife when he describes them as joint-heirs of the grace of life. Priscilla and Aquila were a wonderful example of just such a couple - joint heirs indeed of the grace of life! You never read of them separately. They were always together. Our first introduction to them is when the apostle Paul lived with them at Corinth. They had the same trade as Paul - tent-making - and that brought them together. I've often wondered whether it was during those days in Corinth they first came to know the Lord. If so, they made rapid progress spiritually, for Paul only stayed in Corinth for 18 months. Then he moved on to Ephesus and they went with him. And in Ephesus, where they made their new home, they met Apollos. The Bible describes him as mighty in the Scriptures. But when Aquila and Priscilla heard him preaching in the synagogue they detected he wasn't clear on the difference between John's baptism and the baptism of disciples of the Lord Jesus. So they invited him home and, to use the Bible expression, 'they expounded unto him the way of God more carefully'. It says much for Apollos that he was willing to accept the help they offered, and for them also, that they were able to give it. They used their home in the service of the Lord, as all of us can who have homes. In fact, their home became the meeting place of the church. They were certainly a great couple. Paul refers to them as his fellow-workers in Christ Jesus. He says for his life they laid down their own necks. And not only did he give thanks for them, but so did all the churches of the Gentiles. So as they travelled they came well known, and many had cause to thank God for the help they gave.

SIXTY-EIGHT: TITUS

Titus is one of the better known characters of the New Testament perhaps, for there's an epistle bearing his name. It was written to him by the apostle Paul and he describes Titus as his true child after a common faith. So evidently he'd had the privilege of leading him to Christ. As might be expected a strong bond existed between them, something like a father and son relationship. A younger man serving with an older. We very often find that in the Scriptures. It's an excellent arrangement. The older man is able to pass on the benefit of his experience, and he in turn benefits from the zeal and energy of youth.

Titus is presented as a man of deep feeling. Paul sent him to encourage the disciples in Corinth and it's obvious from what he wrote that Titus was affected by their state. Their sorrows became his sorrows and their joys his joys. It says he was comforted in them, and refreshed by them. Paul spoke about his inward affection being more abundantly toward them. That shows how much they were on his heart. Inward affection is one word in the Greek, and is sometimes translated compassion. You remember it is often said about the Lord Jesus, He was moved with compassion. Well, that's the same word. Titus in this respect had grown like his Master. He was a compassionate man.

Another word which is linked with Titus is earnestness. Twice in 2 Corinthians chapter 8 Paul uses this word to describe him. 'thanks be to God' he says, 'which putteth the same earnest care for you into the heart of Titus'. It's a lovely characteristic. It carries the thought of diligence and haste.

SIXTY-NINE: EPAPHRODITUS

A missionary friend of mine who served the Lord for many years in Nigeria used to tell of a leprous man who insisted on helping him one day when he was travelling through a dangerous part of the bush. He was sadly deformed by the disease but he so much wanted to run ahead to make sure there were no wild animals roaming near the path. When someone asked what he would be able to do anyway, if they did meet any wild beasts, he drew himself to his full height and said 'Have I not a life to give?' Dear man, he had the right spirit, hadn't he?

Epaphroditus whom we read about in the epistle to the Philippians was a man of similar spirit. He was entrusted by the disciples in Philippi to carry their gift to the apostle Paul in Rome and it was a hazardous journey he undertook. Whether he was taken ill on the way or became ill when he arrived is not clear. Certainly he was very sick, near to death, Paul says. But in the mercy of God he recovered and Paul sent him back to the Philippians so that their hearts would rejoice when they saw him again.

And he sent him back with this tremendous commendation, that for the work of Christ he came near to death, hazarding his life. It's a stirring word, isn't it? It was used of those who nursed infected people at great risk to their own lives. That's just what Epaphroditus did - he risked his life. He had given Himself to the Lord Jesus and His service, and whatever that service demanded, he was ready for it, regardless of the cost. No wonder the apostle referred to him so affectionately as 'my brother and fellow- worker and fellow-soldier'. He himself once said 'I hold not my life of any account, as dear unto myself' and that just summed up Epaphroditus' feelings, too. Such men - and women - have caught something of the spirit of their Master. They count it an honour to serve Him, and nothing else matters.

There's only this one reference to Epaphroditus in the Scriptures, but it's such a stirring one we can never forget him. As Longfellow the poet said:

> Lives of great men all remind us
> We can make our lives sublime,
> And departing, leave behind us
> Footprints in the sands of time.

SEVENTY: BURNING HEARTS

'Their eyes were holden that they should not know him' (Luke 24:16). So it says of the two walking to Emmaus when the Stranger drew alongside and companied with them. And when they did eventually recognize Him as He blessed and brake the bread in their home, He vanished out of their sight. So throughout the experience they were unaware of who their Visitor was. At no point did they look upon Him in recognition. Why was that? Why did God withhold from them the joy of recognizing their Master, when their hearts were breaking because of Him? I suggest it was because He wanted to teach them they could no longer depend upon His physical presence with them. Though they had known Christ after the flesh yet now they would know Him so no more.

But His physical presence which they had valued so much was to give place to an enjoyment of Him in the Scriptures. And as they reminisced together after His departure, that was the outstanding memory which lingered with them. 'Was not our heart burning within us' they said, 'while he spake to us in the way, while he opened to us the scriptures?' and 'beginning from Moses and from all the prophets, he interpreted to them in all the scriptures the things concerning himself'. What a tremendous experience!

The journey from Jerusalem to Emmaus was about seven and a half miles and on rough roads it could well have taken three to four hours. They learned that night a lesson they never forgot, that Christ is in all the Scriptures; and as the Holy Spirit operated in their hearts He would make Him as real to them, and as precious, as ever He was when they companied with Him on earth. 'He shall take of mine' He said, speaking of the Comforter who was to come, and 'declare it unto you'. And so He will, not only in their hearts, but in ours also.

This is surely the lesson of the Emmaus road. And it was repeated, only hours later, as He stood in the midst of His apostles and said, 'all things must needs be fulfilled, which are written in the law of Moses, and the prophets, and the psalms, concerning me. Then opened he their mind, that they might understand the scriptures'. May we also have opened minds to see the living Christ in His living Word. But we shall need to muse upon Him, and commune with each other concerning Him, as they did, and then the fire will kindle. And our hearts will burn as the living Christ becomes increasingly real and precious to us in His Word.

SEVENTY-ONE: IN THE BEGINNING

'In the beginning God'. In this majestic way the canon of Scripture opens. They are just simple words in our English language, but placed together by inspiration of the Holy Spirit they convey profound truth to our hearts. 'In the beginning God'. As far back as human minds can go, and further still, God was always there. 'Even from everlasting to everlasting, thou art God', said Moses in the lovely 90th psalm. Think about these words as they apply to our Lord Jesus, for He speaks of Himself in the final chapter of Revelation, 'I am the Alpha and the Omega, the first and the last, the beginning and the end'. As the Father is, so is He.

He is the beginning of all creation. 'All things were made by him; and without him was not anything made that hath been made'. He is the Firstborn of all creation, in the sense that He has priority and precedence above all created beings and things. He is the pre-eminent One, for it was the good pleasure of the Father that in Him should all the fulness dwell. He is the beginning of God's ways, the One in whom all the treasures of wisdom and knowledge are hidden. 'Doth not wisdom cry?' asks king Solomon in the first verse of Proverbs chapter 8, and then he goes on to describe Wisdom personified in God's only Son. 'The LORD possessed me in the beginning of his way'. I love the way Cowper has put it in his poem:

> Ere God had built the mountains,
> Or raised the fruitful hills;
> Before He filled the fountains

That feed the running rills;
In One from everlasting,
The wonderful I AM
Found pleasures never wasting,
And Wisdom was His name.'

He is the beginning of divine revelation. 'In the beginning was the Word, and the Word was with God, and the Word was God'! He is the One through whom God has chosen to express Himself. Having of old time spoken to the fathers in the prophets, He has at the end of these days spoken unto us in His Son. John looked into a future day and he saw the heaven opened and the Lord Jesus coming forth to judge and make war, and His name is called the Word of God.

SEVENTY-TWO: THE CREATOR

In the evening of the day when the Lord Jesus was raised from the dead, two of His followers were walking from Jerusalem to Emmaus. Very sad and disconsolate they were, for their Master had been crucified and buried in a tomb and all their hopes for Him had been shattered. They were talking together about all that had happened, when a Stranger joined them and walked with them. They did not realize who He was until later when they had invited Him into their home and He was revealed to them as He took the bread and gave thanks for it and gave it to them. Then they knew Him and understood how He had thrilled their hearts as He opened the Scriptures to them. Beginning from Moses and all the prophets He interpreted to them in all the Scriptures the things concerning Himself. The books of Moses, of course, are the first five books of our Bible, perhaps the part most under attack by those who take it upon themselves to criticize God's Word. But to those of us who love our Lord Jesus, these books are just full of Himself.

In the very first verse He is present, for it says, 'In the beginning God created the heaven and the earth'. Hebrew scholars tell us that while God is a plural noun, the verb 'created' is in the singular. Certainly the Holy Spirit was there, for the next verse says ' the spirit of God moved upon the face of the waters'. And so was the Lord Jesus, for the apostle John tells us that all things were made by Him; and without Him was not anything made that hath been made.

In the Genesis account we read, 'and God said, Let there be light: and there was light'. It was a word of almighty power. 'He spake, and it was done' said the psalmist, 'He commanded, and it stood fast' (Psalm 33:9). And with that agrees the word in Hebrews chapter 11, 'By faith we understand that the worlds have been framed by the word of God'. It was the Eternal Word who spoke in creative power. 'In the beginning was the Word, and the Word was with God, and the Word was God'. That is one of His glorious titles which He will keep forever. By Him the worlds were brought into being, working together with His Father and the Holy Spirit. He is the great Creator God. Such were some of the great things those two disciples learnt on that unforgettable walk to Emmaus.

SEVENTY-THREE: THE CHURCH, WHICH IS HIS BODY

The Scriptures are full of Christ, and when we love our Lord Jesus it is exciting to find Him on every page of our Bibles. 'Ye search the scriptures' He said to the Jews who did not believe on Him, 'because ye think that in them ye have eternal life; and these are they which bear witness of me'. They failed to find Him in the Scriptures because their hearts were darkened by sin, but when the eyes of our hearts are enlightened Christ shines on every page!

In Genesis chapter 2 there is an arresting word. 'the LORD God said, It is not good that the man should be alone; I will make him an help meet for him'. Everything else in His creation was good and each day He pronounced it so. On the final day 'God saw everything that he had made, and, behold, it was very good'. But one thing was not good: that man should be alone. He needed a help answering to him. And it says, 'the LORD God caused a deep sleep to fall upon the man, and he slept; and he took one of his ribs, and closed up the flesh instead thereof: and the rib, which the LORD God had taken from the man, made he a woman, and brought her unto the man.'

That was the first marriage, beautiful in its simplicity, and God officiated at it. When Adam woke from his sleep, God presented him with his bride, beautiful, perfect from the hand of God. And Adam said, 'This is now bone of my bones, and flesh of my flesh: she shall be called Woman, because she was taken out of Man'.

She belonged to him because she was part of him. She had been taken out of his side. She was literally a member of his body. And so are we who belong to the Lord Jesus. 'we are members of his body' says the apostle in Ephesians chapter 5. 'Christ also loved the church, and gave himself up for it'. He passed through the deep sleep of death that He might have us to be with Him for ever. 'This mystery is great' said the apostle, 'but I speak in regard of Christ and of the church'. It is indeed a great mystery. I am sure the full wonder of it will only be understood when we reach the glory. But this much we can grasp and enjoy right now, that we belong to Christ as surely as Eve belonged to Adam. We have been given to Him by His Father, joined to Him as members of His Body. And we shall be with Him for ever, 'the fulness of him that filleth all in all'.

SEVENTY-FOUR: THE WOMAN'S SEED

When I was in Burma some years ago there was a fine Burmese man in the church who was a retired Inspector of Schools. He had a great love for his Bible. He began studying it when he was a graduate of Rangoon University, and one of his earliest recollections was being taught the first Messianic prophecy. That is the first promise of the Messiah who was to come. He often referred to it and taught us lessons from it. And I would like to share with you some of the lessons I learned from him. The verse is found in Genesis 3 in the portion where God spoke to the serpent and said 'I will put enmity between thee and the woman, and between thy seed and her seed: it shall bruise thy head, and thou shalt bruise his heel'. That is the very first direct reference to the Lord Jesus in our Bibles. He is spoken of as the woman's Seed.

That is a unique expression. In the birth of our Lord Jesus there was no man involved. He was born of a virgin, and God told Mary very plainly how it would happen. 'The Holy Ghost shall come upon thee, and the power of the Most High shall overshadow thee: wherefore also that which is to be born shall be called holy, the Son of God'. Great is the mystery of godliness; He who was manifested in the flesh. And we bow in worship as we ponder the wonderful way in which God's holy Son came into human experience.

And from the beginning the word of God has proved true, that there has been enmity between the Devil and the woman and between his seed and her seed. 'it shall bruise thy head' God said 'and thou shalt bruise his heel'. And that happened, too. At Calvary the Lord Jesus was bruised for our iniquities. But that only for a little while - only His heel, as it were - for He rose again from the dead on the third day, triumphant over all His foes. And the Bible says, in Romans 16, 'the God of peace shall bruise Satan under your feet shortly'.

That day is coming. Satan still has a limited amount of power today, and we are told to be watchful, for our adversary the Devil, as a roaring lion, walks about, seeking whom he may devour. So let us be on our guard, and at the same time thank God that His very first promise about His Son will eventually find its complete fulfilment when the great Deceiver will be cast for ever into the lake of fire and brimstone.

SEVENTY-FIVE: THE LAST ADAM

When the Lord Jesus joined the two who were walking to Emmaus, it says 'beginning from Moses and from all the prophets, he interpreted to them in all the scriptures the things concerning himself'. We have been enjoying together some of the glimpses of Christ we find in the early chapters of Genesis. Adam is presented to us as the first man, and the apostle Paul comments on that fact in his first epistle to the Corinthians, when he says, 'The first man Adam became a living soul. The last Adam became a life-giving spirit'.

So Adam heads up a race of men who receive life as he received it, from the great Creator. But alas, through his disobedience to God's plain word, he passed on to them the awful result of sin, which is death. In Romans 5:12 we read 'through one man sin entered into the world, and death through sin; and so death passed unto all men, for that all sinned'. Adam is described as a figure of Christ, but he stands in contrast to Him. 'The first man is of the earth, earthy: the second man is of heaven'. Adam led men into sin and death, but the Lord Jesus came to suffer death on our behalf, and to lead many sons to glory.

I like the way the apostle Paul puts it in Romans 5:19 'through the one man's disobedience the many were made sinners, even so through the obedience of the one shall the many be made righteous'. How much is contained in those few words. He was always obedient, of course. He delighted to do His Father's will. But in Hebrews 5 we read that He ' learned obedience by the things which he suffered', which I understand to mean that through life's experience of suffering He was constantly learning what obedience cost. He learned it in daily experience. And every suffering He endured resulted in glory to His God and Father in heaven.

Never did obedience cost a man more than it cost the Lord Jesus when He went out from Gethsemane's garden to give Himself upon the Cross. 'nevertheless not my will, but thine, be done' He said, and He went out to become obedient even unto death, yea, the death of the cross. Thank God through His obedience the many have been made righteous, just as many as will receive it by faith. And now He invites us to be obedient to Him, by obeying His commandments and following where He leads the way.

SEVENTY-SIX: GOD'S DESIRE REALIZED

The idea of God dwelling among men on earth first came from His own heart, as was pointed out in the very first issue of Needed Truth, in an article entitled 'Let them make Me a sanctuary'. The title is taken from God's Word to His people after He had redeemed them from Egypt, baptized them to Moses their new leader in the cloud and in the water of the Red Sea, and brought them to mount Sinai where they pledged their obedience to all that He commanded. Then God said, and not before, 'let them make me a sanctuary; that I may dwell among them' (Exodus 25:8). At His invitation the willing-hearted brought their gifts in lavish abundance and the wise-hearted used them according to the pattern Moses had received from God. The result was a movable tabernacle in which God was pleased to dwell, and the people of Israel had the unique privilege of pitching their tents around God's Tent, and having the eternal God dwelling in their midst.

Later Solomon built Him a magnificent temple which was to human eyes at any rate, more worthy of Jehovah God than the movable tabernacle, but Solomon asked in wonder 'will God in very deed dwell with men on the earth?' (2 Chronicles 6:18). The amazement Solomon expressed has been shared by many down the centuries, for the contemplation is overwhelming. If heaven and the heaven of heavens cannot contain Him, how much less any house men might build, whether material as in past ages, or spiritual today. Yet He desires to dwell among men on earth. Such is the heart of our God.

SEVENTY-SEVEN: THE AMEN

I was visiting Niagara recently with a friend, and was impressed all over again by the sound of many waters as they hurled themselves over the Horseshoe Falls. And spanning the waters in the sky was the most beautiful rainbow, shining brightly in all its colours. I am told the rainbow can be seen any day between 2 and 4 p.m. when the sun is shining. I went back to my Bible to read about the first time God put His bow in the cloud. It was after the Flood, you remember, when Noah came out of the ark, that God made a covenant with all mankind that while the earth remains, seedtime and harvest, cold and heat, summer and winter, day and night, shall not cease. And then He said 'I do set my bow in the cloud, and it shall be for a token of a covenant between me and the earth' (Genesis 9:13). It was something men could look at, and remember that God always keeps His promises.

But more than that - and I had not noticed this before - it was something for God to look at, too. 'the bow shall be in the cloud; and I will look upon it' He said, 'that I may remember the everlasting covenant'. So that bow in the cloud which many thousands of tourists to Niagara gaze upon every year is seen also by God in heaven - a reminder to Him and to us that His Word can never fail. He always keeps His promises. So every time you see the rainbow in the sky, yes, and even when you do not, remember that Father, Son and Holy Spirit are all pledged to make sure to us the promises with which Scripture abounds. Oh how favoured we are!

SEVENTY-EIGHT: GOD'S BELOVED SON

Genesis chapter 5 gives us the generations of Adam through to the days of Noah, and of each of the men mentioned, except one, it says '... and he died'. Those words run like a refrain through the whole chapter: '... and he died'. As though God would impress upon us for all time that the Devil is a liar from the beginning, for you remember he told Eve, 'Ye shall not surely die'. But he was wrong, as this chapter makes abundantly clear. One generation of men after another lived, begat sons and daughters, and then they died, with the exception of one man. It is recorded, 'Enoch walked with God: and he was not; for God took him'. The eleventh chapter of Hebrews has a fine commentary on that. It says, 'By faith Enoch was translated that he should not see death; and he was not found, because God translated him: for before his translation he hath had witness borne to him that he had been well-pleasing unto God.'

We also make it our aim to be well-pleasing unto Him, wrote the apostle Paul to the Corinthians, but how? Surely in the same way as Enoch did - Enoch walked with God. What was involved in that, we may ask? Well, there must have been agreement for, 'Shall two walk together, except they have agreed?' asks Amos the prophet. Enoch must have agreed with God that he would walk where God led the way. And then step by step and day by day he kept to his promise and walked in fellowship with God. And God bore witness to him that he had been well-pleasing to Him.

SEVENTY-NINE: THE LAMB OF GOD

In the third chapter of Genesis some of the awful consequences of sin are presented to us. For instance, the way to the garden of Eden was closed to Adam and his wife, guarded by the cherubim with flaming sword. But while the book of Genesis presents the beginnings of human experience, the book of Revelation presents the end of it, at least the end of what is recorded, and it is interesting and thrilling to compare the third chapter of Genesis with the final two chapters of Revelation. For instance, the gates of the eternal city are for ever open. And the way to the tree of life which was barred when Adam sinned is now open to all who have washed their robes, for they have the right to come to the tree of life and to enter in by the gates to the city. In Genesis 3 the curse is imposed. But in Revelation chapter 22 verse 3 it says, 'there shall be no curse any more'. Then again, sorrow and death came in through sin, but both are abolished when you come to Revelation 21. God says 'death shall be no more' and 'he shall wipe away every tear from their eyes', and moreover there will be no mourning, nor crying, nor pain any more, for these are the first things, and they are passed away for ever.

God's fellowship with His creatures was interrupted on account of sin. No longer could He come to talk with Adam in the garden. And there is no doubt that God felt that loss more keenly than ever Adam did. But when you turn to Revelation 21, all that God lost is restored, for the tabernacle of God is with men, and ' they shall be his peoples, and God himself shall be with them, and be their God'.

But why so great a change? Between the books of Genesis and the Revelation comes the story of the Saviour's life and death and of His glorious resurrection. He is the Lamb of God foretold in Genesis, and He bore the sin of the world when He gave Himself in death at Calvary. And in the Revelation He is seen in all His glory as the Lamb standing in the midst of the throne. The throne of God and of the Lamb is the very centre of the eternal city and out of it proceeds the river of water of life, bright as crystal. So while death came in as a result of sin in the book of Genesis and produced its awful trail throughout the Bible record, by the close of God's revelation we see sin and death conquered for ever and the Lord Jesus is triumphant over all.

EIGHTY: CHILDREN OF GOD

When a person believes in the Lord Jesus he is born again and becomes a child of God. This new birth is the work of the Holy Spirit using the incorruptible seed of the Word of God and as a result the believer becomes a partaker of the divine nature (1 Pet.1:23; 2 Pet.1:4). That is why John says so plainly 'Whosoever is begotten of God doeth no sin, because his seed abideth in him: and he cannot sin, because he is begotten of God' (1 Jn 3:9). It is the new nature in us which does not sin. It cannot sin for it is God's nature, and it follows therefore that, possessing it, we cannot be lost. There is a part of us, of course, which is very liable to sin, and John speaks about that also. 'If we say we have no sin, we deceive ourselves, and the truth is not in us' (1 Jn 1:8). We have to understand the two lines of truth and rightly divide between them. But we can see that having become a child of God we cannot cease to be part of God's family. When God becomes our heavenly Father and we His children it is in a relationship which cannot be broken. How we behave as His children is another matter about which the Bible has much to say. It speaks of reward for those who love Christ and serve Him faithfully; and it speaks also of loss to those whose works are burned up at the judgement seat of Christ. That is where the assessment of our works will be made and we must each stand before His judgement seat. 1 Cor.3:13-15 speaks about it, and please notice carefully v.15, 'If any man's work shall be burned, he shall suffer loss: but he himself shall be saved; yet so as through fire'. Notice the distinction between himself and his works. It is the works that are burned; the man himself is saved, for a child of God cannot be lost. Reward and loss have to do with service and not with our eternal life.

EIGHTY-ONE: JEREMIAH'S CALL

The days were hard when Jeremiah was called to serve. God told him even when He appointed him to His service that the people would not listen to his message. Their hearts were stubbornly set to go their own way and God knew it, but before His judgement fell He must warn them again of the consequences of their sin. So once again God spoke to them, and whenever He speaks He looks for a man to be His mouthpiece, and the man this time was Jeremiah.

Jeremiah prophesied through the reign of five kings, although only three are mentioned in the opening verses of his book, for the other two reigned for only three months each. Although the majority of the nation had turned away from God there were still some who feared the Lord, and Jeremiah belonged to such a family. His father was Hilkiah who may well have been the high priest who discovered the book of the law in the house of God in the reign of Josiah. A comparison of chapter 32:7 with 2 Chronicles 34:22 suggests that Shallum the husband of Huldah the prophetess may have been Jeremiah's uncle. So he was brought up in godly surroundings among people who feared the Lord. He must surely have felt the influence of their lives, and early in his own life he set his heart to serve the Lord. When God is looking for a man to speak His word He looks for one who has become familiar with His voice in the secret place, and I am sure that Jeremiah was such a man. He was young, perhaps in his late teens or early twenties, when the word of God came to him, and this is how he spoke about his experience:

'The word of the LORD came to me, saying, "Before I formed you in the womb

I knew you, before you were born I set you apart; I appointed you as a prophet to the nations." "Ah, Sovereign LORD," I said, "I do not know how to speak; I am only a child."' (Jeremiah 1:4-6 NIV).

What a tremendous word to come to a young man. His response shows the deep impact that it had upon him. He was overwhelmed by the solemnity of it. 'Ah Sovereign LORD,' he said, 'I do not know how to speak.' He did not say, 'I will not speak', but 'I do not know how to speak'. It was a cry of weakness rather than unwillingness. Indeed even as he protested, he declared his willingness by the very title he used in speaking to God. The Sovereign Jehovah, the mighty God, the eternal Jehovah was his supreme Lord, and Jeremiah had already learned that there was no arguing with Him. He felt utterly unable for the task – overwhelmed by the awesomeness of it – but he was not refusing to obey. God loves men like that: men who feel their deep weakness, but are willing to put their trust in Him.

EIGHTY-TWO: MY WORDS IN YOUR MOUTH

Shortly before the Second World War a Bible distributor visited a small town in Poland and gave a Bible to a man who was converted through reading it. Bibles were in short supply, so the new believer passed it on to others with the same glorious effect that they were also drawn to Christ. That process continued until that one Bible had been used in the conversion of two hundred persons.

What a power there is in the Word of God. It 'is living, and active, and sharper than any two-edged sword' (Hebrews 4:12). Jeremiah found that to be so, and he was called to a lifetime of speaking God's word. When God first called him he protested for he felt completely unable for the task. 'I cannot speak,' he said, 'for I am a child' (Jeremiah 1:6). God's answer was to put forth His hand and touch Jeremiah's mouth. 'Behold, I have put my words in thy mouth', said God (Jeremiah 1:9). Ah, that is the answer, not only for Jeremiah, but for all who are called upon to speak God's word. May God save us from the error of speaking our own words and teach us to wait on Him in the secret place until we feel His touch, and He puts His words in our mouths. This is so important, for we are living in a world which is hungry for the authoritative preaching of the Word of God.

EIGHTY-THREE: SPEAK MY WORD

'Is not my word like as fire? saith the LORD; and like a hammer that breaketh the rock in pieces?' (Jeremiah 23:29). Have you felt the power of the Word of God in your life? Have you felt it hammering away at your heart until you have been forced to face up to what God is saying to you? That is the way God brings blessing into our lives.

God told Jeremiah the Word of God through him would be for breaking down and building up, and so it will be in our lives, breaking down the things that are wrong and building up what is right and true and for the glory of God. Let us have hearts to do what God says to us in His Word, and not be a hearer that forgets, but a doer that works, and we shall be blessed in the doing (James 1:25). Then, as we are obedient to the Word ourselves, let us speak it out to others. Let the preachers give themselves to their preaching. The exhortation that Paul gave to Timothy was: 'Preach the Word; be prepared in season and out of season; correct, rebuke and encourage - with great patience and careful instruction' (2 Timothy 4:2 NIV). We are not all called to the public platform, but we are all responsible to speak God's Word at every opportunity that comes our way. 'he that hath my word, let him speak my word faithfully' (Jeremiah 23:28). Jeremiah has shown us the way, let us follow his example.

EIGHTY-FOUR: LIVING WATER

Who would choose stagnant water out of a cistern in preference to fresh water from a spring? That is what Israel did, and God tells us about it in Jeremiah chapter 2. It is a story of wounded love. God had loved them with an everlasting love and drawn them with lovingkindness, but they had forsaken Him. Recounting it God said: 'For my people have committed two evils; they have forsaken me the fountain of living waters, and hewed them out cisterns, broken cisterns, that can hold no water' (Jeremiah 2:13). They turned away from God, the fountain of living water, and dug out for themselves cisterns to gather their own water supply. That would have been folly enough had their own cisterns been able to hold water, but they were not, for they were broken cisterns that very soon ran dry.

The world has many cisterns too, from which the Devil invites us to draw. Cisterns of pleasure, of sport, of wealth and fame, but they are all broken cisterns. They seem to satisfy for a little while, but they soon run dry and the soul is left unsatisfied and sad. On the last and great day of the feast of tabernacles the Lord Jesus stood and cried: 'If any man thirst, let him come unto me, and drink' (John 7:37).

It is a message that runs through the Scriptures. Some seven centuries before the Lord Jesus came to live amongst us, Isaiah cried: 'Ho, every one that thirsteth, come ye to the waters, and he that hath no money; come ye, buy, and eat; yea, come, buy wine and milk without money and without price' (Isaiah 55:1). And on the very last page of our Bibles is the invitation: 'And he that is athirst, let him come: he that will, let him take the water of life freely' (Revelation 22:17). God knows our hearts are thirsty. He made us that way. We have been made by Him and for Him, and the thirst of our hearts can only be satisfied in Him. There is no other place where the thirst of human hearts can be quenched. The psalmist said: 'They shall be abundantly satisfied, For with thee is the fountain of life' (Psalm 36:8,9).

EIGHTY-FIVE: THE KNOWLEDGE OF GOD

Thus saith the LORD, 'Let not the wise man glory in his wisdom, neither let the mighty man glory in his might, let not the rich man glory in his riches: but let him that glorieth glory in this, that he understandeth, and knoweth me, that I am the LORD which exercise lovingkindness, judgement, and righteousness, in the earth: for in these things I delight, saith the LORD' (Jeremiah 9:23,24).

If God had written these words today, then they could not have been more up-to-date. These are the very things that men boast in today, the things that occupy so much of their attention -wisdom, knowledge and education, might and power and the influence that goes with it, riches and wealth and all the material things that wealth can buy. These are the things which dominate the lives of so many people in our world. 'What is wrong with them?' you may ask; nothing, as far as they go. Wisdom, strength and riches are all gifts from God, so certainly there is nothing wrong with them. But God says we are not to boast in them - in other words, we are not to set our hearts on them.

There are two simple reasons why we should not do so. The first is that these things are all of limited value and the second, they are all passing away. We cannot take them with us when the time comes for us to leave this world. There are things in life which are far more important than these three things put together, and God names them for us, lovingkindness, judgement and righteousness. These are the things He delights in and which He is working out in our world today. Lovingkindness is God's love in action, stooping down to men in their need. Judgement or justice is the administration of human affairs in equity and truth. Righteousness is that which is absolutely true and straight and devoid of perversity or crookedness. God delights in these things.

Let us pause for a moment to consider what sort of world this would be if these three things prevailed. There would be no wars or fighting, no greed and hatred, no violence and brutality, no oppression of the poor or neglect of the handicapped and elderly. We can understand why God delights in these things. Honest men and women are striving after them, but they elude us, and will continue to do so until the Lord Jesus comes and sets up His kingdom.

EIGHTY-SIX: THE POTTER'S HOUSE

'Arise, and go down to the potter's house, and there I will cause thee to hear my words. Then I went down to the potter's house, and, behold, he wrought his work on the wheels' (Jeremiah 18:2,3). We can picture the scene as Jeremiah stood in the potter's house and watched him at his work. But it was not a question of interest merely; God had a lesson for him to learn from the potter and it is one which applies to us also. A key text in Isaiah helps us to understand the point that is being made. The prophet says: 'But now, O LORD, thou art our father; we are the clay, and thou our potter; and we all are the work of thy hand' (Isaiah 64:8). God is the Potter and we are the clay, and He is working in our lives, if we allow Him, to make us into vessels that He can use in His service and for His glory. Paul describes it to Timothy: 'a vessel unto honour, sanctified, meet for the master's use, prepared unto every good work' (2 Timothy 2:21). With these verses in mind let us consider the message God had for Jeremiah and learn the lesson of the potter's house. We would agree at the beginning that before the potter commences his work he has a plan in mind. He can see in his mind's eye the vessel he is about to make. And God has a plan in His mind as He works in our lives. In Jeremiah chapter 29 He states this clearly: '"For I know the plans I have for you," declares the LORD, "plans to prosper you and not to harm you, plans to give you hope and a future"' (Jeremiah 29:11 NIV). That is a particularly precious verse. If we link it with Ephesians 2:10 we can see that God had a plan in mind long before He started working on us, for there Paul says: 'For we are his workmanship, created in Christ Jesus for good works, which God afore prepared that we should walk in them'.

EIGHTY-SEVEN: THE POTTER AND THE CLAY

It is wonderful to realize that before we were born God had His plan for us, and now that we are saved He is working out that plan in our lives, or at least He wants to if we will allow Him. His plan for each one of us is different. He does not make two vessels alike. If each blade of grass is different, and no two snowflakes are exactly alike, we can be perfectly sure that when God works in human lives He produces in each one of us His own unique work of art. What a wonderful contemplation! God at work in our lives to produce in us something for His glory and usefulness - vessels suitable for our heavenly Father's use. But how does He do it? Ah, we must watch the potter at his work to see that two things are involved. There is the turning of the wheel and the skilful hands of the potter. The potter places the lump of soft clay on the revolving wheel and then under his hands the vessel takes shape. The turning wheel and the skilful hands produce the desired result. Is that not the way the divine Potter deals with us? On the wheel of life He works; in the continuous round of daily experience His hands are upon us, applying a little pressure here and a little pressure there until He shapes us into a vessel that He can use. But we have to be willing to respond to the pressure of His hands. The pressure takes different forms, of course; sometimes it comes in the discipline that is referred to in Hebrews chapter 12, and the secret of benefiting from such discipline is to be exercised by it, to accept it as God's training for us. The apostle Paul sums it all up when he asks, 'hath not the potter a right over the clay?' (Romans 9:21). That question goes to the heart of the matter.

EIGHTY-EIGHT: THE NEW COVENANT

Very often God reserves His brightest promises for the darkest days. It was so in the case of the promise God spoke through Jeremiah when the Babylonian army was mustering outside the city of Jerusalem, ready to destroy it and to carry its people away into captivity because of their repeated disobedience. The outlook could hardly have been darker, and it was then that God gave them, like a shaft of light, His most wonderful promise. Here it is: 'Behold, the days come, saith the LORD, that I will make a new covenant with the house of Israel, and with the house of Judah: not according to the covenant that I made with their fathers in the day that I took them by the hand to bring them out of the land of Egypt; but this is the covenant that I will make ... I will put my law in their inward parts, and in their heart will I write it; and I will be their God, and they shall be my people: and they shall teach no more every man his neighbour, and every man his brother, saying, Know the LORD: for they shall all know me, from the least of them unto the greatest of them, saith the LORD: for I will forgive their iniquity, and their sin will I remember no more' (Jeremiah 31:31–34).

These are remarkable words, and they are quoted in full in Hebrews chapter 8, for the day is coming when God will completely fulfil this promise and take up Israel once again as His people. So many portions of the Word of God speak of those great days that are coming for Israel. But that is not all, for if you turn over to chapter 10 of Hebrews you will find that this same promise has its application to us today. 'And the Holy Ghost also beareth witness to us: for after he hath said, This is the covenant that I will make with them ... then saith he, And their sins and their iniquities will I remember no more' (vv. 15-17). These are great words and they are written to us, as the Holy Spirit bears witness.

EIGHTY-NINE: THE FIELD IN ANATHOTH

'How can I be sure of God's will in the big decisions of life?' That is a question that is often asked. Every one of us who loves the Lord Jesus wants to be sure that we are doing what pleases Him when it comes to making decisions which will affect the whole course of our lives. But how can we be sure?

There is an incident in the life of Jeremiah which helps us on this point. It is found in Jeremiah chapter 32. Jeremiah was shut up in prison at the time, for king Zedekiah did not like the message that he was bringing from the Lord. For forty years Jeremiah had been warning Judah of God's coming judgement on account of their sin, and now his words were coming to pass, for the army of Babylon was surrounding Jerusalem, and the people could not get in or out.

At that very point in time, when the overthrow of the city was imminent, God spoke to Jeremiah and told him to buy a field in his home town of Anathoth. Jeremiah was greatly perplexed, God had said that they were going into captivity for seventy years; surely it was no time for buying a field. Was it really God who was speaking to him, or had he been mistaken? That was the question. Jeremiah was not sure. Sometimes we are brought into situations where we are faced with big decisions and we are not sure which way to go.

In Jeremiah's case he was given clear guidance by God, for a short time after God had spoken to him his uncle's son came to him with the proposal that he buy the field just as God said he should. Then Jeremiah knew that the word was indeed from the Lord, the circumstances had confirmed it. Is not that often the case in our own experience? When the following four things work together we may be fairly sure that God is leading us on. Firstly there is the inclination of the heart brought about, either by some word from God through the Scriptures, or by some urge that the Holy Spirit brings. Secondly as we pray about it circumstances appear to tie in.

Thirdly, and this is important, we seek the advice of other Christian friends, those who have passed through life's experiences with the Lord, and whose advice we can trust. It is important to share with others the big decisions of life, and be guided by their counsel, rather than go it alone. During all the time we are considering the matter we should continue to make it the subject of our daily prayers. Fourthly, and finally, in response to prayer there comes an answer of peace to the heart. If there is a sincere desire on our part to take God's way and not our own way He will surely not allow us to make any serious mistakes if we follow these steps.

NINETY: THE RECHABITES

We read about the Rechabites in Jeremiah chapter 35. But the man who made them famous was called Jonadab who gave commandment to his sons and daughters that they should drink no wine, build no houses, but live in tents, sow no seed and plant no vineyards. His instructions seemed to be very severe, and we might argue that he was depriving them of perfectly legitimate things.

However, it is obvious that he was a man who feared God deeply, and seeing the awful wickedness around him he desired to preserve his posterity from such sin and lawlessness, and so he placed them under this solemn pledge. It was calculated to preserve their pilgrim character and keep them from putting down roots. The great founders of the nation of Israel had been pilgrims who lived in tents, and Jonadab decided that his family should do the same. The remarkable thing is that 250 years later his descendants were absolutely true to this family tradition, and that is what it was. A tradition is something handed down from one generation to another, and from one generation to another they had passed it on and had lived by it. Jeremiah did not want to tempt the Rechabites into disloyalty to their pledge; he wanted to use the example of their devotion as an object lesson for God's people, Judah. The Rechabites had been far more true to the commandments of their forefathers than Judah had been to the commandments of the Lord. That is the main point that comes out of the story to provide a lesson for us today.

Let us think for a moment about the power of tradition. You may have your own thoughts about the demands that Jonadab placed on his family and whether he was asking more than was reasonable, but perhaps you will agree that if the demands kept them from sin and resulted in a closer walk with God there was profit in them. They also illustrate the amazing power of tradition, for after some 250 years Jonadab's descendants were still keeping strictly to the details of his instructions. There is no doubt that men love to be loyal to tradition. Is that a good thing or a bad thing? It depends on whether or not the traditions are according to God's Word. The Lord Jesus had stern words for the Pharisees about their traditions because they cut right across the clear commandments of God.

On the other hand there were traditions which the apostles urged the disciples to keep because they were based on God's Word. Paul, writing to the church of God in Corinth, commended them for their observance of such traditions (1 Corinthians 11:2). So this is a point of real interest to us all, for tradition dies hard as we have seen. Are you and I bound by any tradition in our family lives or in our church associations? That is a question worth asking ourselves, and if we are, let us check them out with God's Word to make sure that they are not cutting across any plain commandment of the Lord.

NINETY-ONE: BURNING THE ROLL

Have you ever read the story of how we got our English Bible? It is an enthralling story of men who gave all that they had, and even life itself - to bring the Word of God to us in our own mother tongue. William Tyndale was perhaps the foremost of the pioneers, and one day he said to the local clergy, 'If God give me life, 'ere many years the ploughboys shall know more of the Scriptures than you do'. But it cost him his life to do it. The invention of the printing machine greatly helped him, of course, but the opposition to his work was almost unbelievable. At one time his antagonists bought every copy of the Scriptures that they could find and burned them at St Paul's. But with the money received, Tyndale was able to publish copies of the Scriptures cheaply and in clear print, and so the Word of God prevailed. It must do, of course, for it is God's living Word, and He plainly says, 'the word of the Lord abideth for ever' (1 Peter 1:25).

Burning copies of God's Word was not new. King Jehoiakim did the very same thing (Jeremiah chapter 36). God spoke His words to Jeremiah, and Baruch his scribe wrote them down on a roll as Jeremiah dictated it to him. Then Jeremiah told Baruch to go and stand at a busy thoroughfare leading to God's house and read the words to the people as they passed by. This was done at an especially busy time in Jerusalem, a day of a Fast, and crowds of people heard the words God had spoken through Jeremiah. Among those who heard them was a young man called Micaiah, and he passed the word to the princes, who were so concerned about the judgement Jeremiah predicted that they reported the words to the king.

He was not satisfied in hearing about it by word of mouth; he commanded them to bring the roll and read it to him. It was winter time, and he was sitting in his winter house warming himself before a fire. It is a vivid picture that the scripture presents to us of the godless king surrounded by his princes, all with solemn faces because of the seriousness of the words they were hearing. The king, snatching his knife, hacked through three or four columns of the roll and threw them into the fire. Three of his princes were horrified and tried to persuade him not to do it, but he just continued in his anger until the whole of the roll was destroyed. And the scripture says that they were not afraid, neither the king nor any of his servants.

The Lord Jesus said, 'Heaven and earth shall pass away, but my words shall not pass away' (Matthew 24:35), and that applies to all of God's Word. Men may destroy copies of it, but the living Word itself can never be destroyed. God told Jeremiah to write again on another roll all the former words and to them were added pronouncements of judgement on Jehoiakim which in due course were fulfilled. Men are still bent on destroying God's Word, not burning it now, at any rate not often, but in more sophisticated ways they are destroying it.

NINETY-TWO: GOD'S WORD - THE ANVIL

Today we frequently find men and women taking it upon themselves to criticize God's Word; they hack away large portions of it by casting doubt on its truthfulness. Have nothing to do with such error. Stand firmly and bravely, if need be, for the truth of God's Word in its entirety, for the whole of it is divinely inspired. Men have been attacking it for centuries, but it stands firm like a rock. A poet has written:

> Last eve I passed beside the blacksmith's door
> And heard the anvil ring the vesper chime;
> When looking down, I saw upon the floor
> Old hammers worn with use in former time.
> How many anvils have you used' said I,
> 'To wear and batter all these hammers so?'
> 'Just one!' said he, and then, with twinkling eye,
> 'The anvil wears the hammers out, you know.'
> Just so, thought I, the anvil of God's Word
> For ages sceptic blows have beat upon;
> Yet, though the noise of falling blows was heard,
> The anvil is unharmed—the hammers gone.' (Source unknown)

How very true. No harm can come to the Word of God; it is safe in God's keeping, but great harm comes to those who refuse its words. Jehoiakim found that to his cost, and so will all those who refuse to receive God's Word into their hearts. The Lord Jesus spoke very solemn words when He said: 'He that rejecteth me, and receiveth not my sayings, hath one that judgeth him: the word that I spake, the same shall judge him in the last day' (John 12:48).

NINETY-THREE: ZEDEKIAH

Our spiritual life and progress depends upon our obedience to the Word of God. We can hardly over-emphasize the importance of such obedience, for it is written on almost every page of our Bibles.

Zedekiah was the last of Judah's kings. During his reign the people were carried into captivity, and he among them. He was a weak sort of man ruled by his princes rather than ruling himself. One time when his princes requested that Jeremiah should be put to death, he replied, 'Behold, he is in your hand: for the king is not he that can do anything against you' (Jeremiah 38:5). But weak as he was he understood the value of God's Word, and deep in his heart he respected God's prophet. One day in his distress he sent secretly for Jeremiah, who was then in prison, and asked, 'Is there any word from the LORD?' And the answer was 'There is' (Jeremiah 37:17). At another secret meeting Jeremiah pleaded with him: 'Obey, I beseech thee, the voice of the LORD, in that which I speak unto thee: so shall it be well with thee, and thy soul shall live' (Jeremiah 38:20).

This is where Zedekiah failed; he wanted to know what God had to say, he valued His Word to that extent, but he was not prepared to obey it. What God asked him to do cut across his own desires, and he chose his own way rather than God's. The last picture that we have of him is pathetic. He was taken captive by Nebuchadnezzar the Babylonian king; his sons were put to death before his eyes, then his eyes were put out and he was bound in fetters and carried into Babylon. What a fearful penalty to pay for disobedience. God has put that sad story on the page of His Word so that we shall be warned by it.

In Jeremiah chapter 17 we read these words: 'Blessed is the man that trusteth in the LORD, and whose hope the LORD is. For he shall be as a tree planted by the waters, and that spreadeth out his roots by the river, and shall not fear when heat cometh, but his leaf shall be green; and shall not be careful in the year of drought, neither shall cease from yielding fruit' (vv.7,8).

NINETY-FOUR: ELIJAH - HIS BACKGROUND

Elijah was a unique man, introduced to us in 1 Kings chapter 17 without any record of his parents or his tribe. We are simply told he was a Tishbite from the mountainous country of Gilead which is on the east side of the Jordan. That part of the land belonged to Manasseh and Gad, so possibly he came from one of those tribes. And he had a nature which seemed to correspond with the rugged hills from which he came. His name is remarkable too. My God is Jah is its meaning, and surely God must have guided his parents when they chose such a name for their boy. On Gilead's hills, maybe as a youth, he decided he was going to live up to his name and he presented himself to God. To that point we must all come if we wish to be used by God. In the spirit of Paul's entreaty in Romans 12 we present our bodies a living sacrifice, holy, acceptable to God. Elijah did just that, and God took him at his word and used him in an outstanding way.

Let us remind ourselves of the days in which he lived. We first read of him during the reign of wicked king Ahab. About 60 years before, when Rehoboam came to the throne, the kingdom was divided into two tribes and ten. Rehoboam was king over the tribes of Judah and Benjamin, and God raised up Jeroboam to be king over the ten tribes of Israel. But he was not a good king. Time and again the divine record says he made Israel to sin. He introduced a spurious worship setting up a golden calf in the north and south of his land and he persuaded his people to worship in these places rather than going to God's house in Jerusalem. He was afraid, of course, that if they went into Judah's territory to worship he might lose them altogether. He set a bad example and the kings who followed him in quick succession were all wicked men, and Ahab was the worst; God distinctly says so. He married Jezebel who was the daughter of the king of the Zidonians and she was even more wicked than her husband. Through her influence the worship of Baal was introduced and this idol worship led Israel far away from God.

It was during Ahab's reign that a man called Hiel rebuilt the city of Jericho against God's explicit instructions. Did he not know what God had said? Surely he did, but he chose to ignore it, and his attitude was characteristic of those days. They were rebellious days. The people were going their own way and deliberately defying God and His Word. The result was fearful sin, such as God must judge. He therefore chose Elijah from the hills of Gilead to be His mouthpiece.

NINETY-FIVE: ELIJAH AT CHERITH'S BROOK

'Now I know that thou art a man of God, and that the word of the LORD in thy mouth is truth' (1 Kings 17:24).

So said the widow woman to Elijah when he brought her dead son to life. He had lived with this woman and her son, so they had had plenty of opportunity to observe his way of life, and this was her conclusion. Elijah was a man of God. What makes a man a man of God? What was there about Elijah that made him answer to this title? When he went to speak to king Ahab he described himself as a man who stood before the Lord. The angel who spoke to Zacharias said, 'I am Gabriel, that stand in the presence of God' (Luke 1:19), and Elijah did the same, waiting the divine command, ready to speak what God said and ready to go wherever God sent. That is what makes a man a man of God.

Away in the hills of Gilead Elijah heard of the fearful sin of God's people the other side of Jordan and his spirit was burdened about it. God's name was being dishonoured and Elijah decided the time had come when something must be done about it. God had plainly said 'Take heed to yourselves, lest your heart be deceived, and ye turn aside, and serve other gods, and worship them; and the anger of the LORD be kindled against you, and he shut up the heaven, that there be no rain, and that the land yield not her fruit' (Deuteronomy 11:16,17).

The days in which he lived answered exactly to that description and Elijah knew that God must be true to His Word, that the rain must be withheld until His people turned to Him in repentance. So he began to pray. James tells us that. We would not know, apart from the word in James chapter 5, that Elijah prayed fervently that it might not rain, and it did not rain on the earth for three years and six months.

Having received the assurance that God had heard his prayer, he then went boldly to king Ahab with his message, 'there shall not be dew nor rain these years, but according to my word'. He knew only too well that Jezebel had put some of the prophets of the Lord to death but at this time he was fearless. 'As the LORD, the God of Israel, liveth' (v.1) was his word, and therein lay his strength. God was still alive despite the fact that all but seven thousand of Israel's people worshipped Baal, and He was still their God.

NINETY-SIX: ELIJAH AT CARMEL

'How long halt ye between two opinions?' was the question with which Elijah challenged the people of Israel when he gathered them on Mount Carmel (1 Kings 18:21). They were all there, the king and his people, 450 prophets of Baal and 400 prophets of Asherah, all gathered at the word of Elijah. The angel Gabriel spoke to Zacharias about the spirit and power of Elijah, and it was remarkably demonstrated at Carmel, for they obeyed his word without dispute.

Maybe the people expected he would give them rain, but before the rain could come sin had to be judged. For years they had yielded lip service to God but in their hearts they were idol-worshippers and the long years of drought had not changed them. So the call rang out 'How long halt ye between two opinions?' The word could be translated 'to totter' like a drunken man whose feet go first one way and then another. That is how His people had been behaving, like the double-minded man whom James speaks about, unstable in all his ways. But God cannot be satisfied with that. He is a jealous God and He claims, and deserves, the undivided loyalty of our hearts. The people had no answer to Elijah's challenge, so he proposed they build two altars and offer two bullocks, and let them call on their gods, and he would call on the living God, and the God who answered by fire, let him be God.

Elijah knew his God. Elijah was confident that in response to his prayer, God would answer by fire. The prophets of Baal went first for they were many, and although they called on the name of Baal from morning to noon there was no answer. Elijah mocked them, but it made no difference when they slashed themselves with knives until the blood flowed. Of course not! For the gods they served had ears which could not hear.

Then it was Elijah's turn. The people watched intently as he took twelve stones, one for each tribe, and with them he built an altar in the Name of the Lord. Around it he dug a trench which was filled with water and the bullock cut in pieces on the altar was drenched with water also. It was the time of evening sacrifice as Elijah stepped forward to pray 'O LORD, the God of Abraham, of Isaac, and of Israel' reminding them of God's promises to their forefathers and to them as a nation. God was a covenant- keeping God. He never failed to keep His promises and on that ground Elijah now called upon Him. His Name had been greatly dishonoured in Israel, a fact which he deeply lamented, and he now called on God to clear His Name of all dishonour. That was the great burden of his heart, that God's Name would be glorified.

NINETY-SEVEN: ELIJAH PRAYING FOR RAIN

On Mount Carmel Elijah stood boldly before the people as he urged God's claims upon them. But later when he climbed to the top of the mountain he was no longer pleading with men, but with God, and he bowed himself to the ground with his face between his knees. That praying man has much to teach us about the important subject of prayer, and the first lesson is the basic one that we have to ask to receive. James comments on this experience in Elijah's life, and reveals that it was because of Elijah's prayer that God withheld the rain in the first place. And then he adds, 'he prayed again; and the heaven gave rain, and the earth brought forth her fruit' (James 5:18).

But God had already promised the rain. That was the message he sent to Ahab, 'I will send rain upon the earth'. Why then did Elijah need to pray for it? The answer is that it is a principle with God that He gives in answer to our prayers. 'Ask, and it shall be given you' the Lord Jesus taught, 'for every one that asketh receiveth' (Matthew 7:7,8). Conversely James says 'ye have not, because ye ask not' (James 4:2). That's a heart-searching word and we might well ask ourselves if it is true in our lives. Is God's blessing being withheld simply because we have not learned the importance of asking in prayer? The precious and exceeding great promises of God which fill our Bibles are to be claimed by faith and prayer. God is honoured when we reverently remind Him of them and claim them through the prayer of faith.

NINETY-EIGHT: WATCH AND PRAY

Elijah sought the solitude of the mountain top to be alone with God, reminding us the Lord Jesus said 'when thou prayest, enter into thine inner chamber, and having shut thy door, pray to thy Father which is in secret, and thy Father which seeth in secret shall recompense thee' (Matthew 6:6). How important that we make time in our busy days for the secret place if we are going to be strong to serve the Lord.

Elijah prayed specifically. He asked that it might not rain and then just as definitely, three and a half years later, he asked God to send the rain. There is no doubt that God wants us to come to Him with our specific requests, and sometimes He lays burdens upon our hearts, so that we shall come to Him, pouring out our hearts for those very things.

Then we find that Elijah prayed fervently. He prayed with prayer, the margin of the Revised Version says. He was deeply in earnest about it. There are degrees of earnestness, for it says about our Lord Jesus in Gethsemane's garden that being in an agony He prayed more earnestly. Prayer was made earnestly by the Church in Jerusalem when Peter was in prison: the word means 'to stretch out' like a piece of elastic. It's wonderful when we are so burdened about what we are asking for that our hearts reach out to God in deep earnestness.

Elijah prayed in faith. That is clear because each time he prayed he sent his servant to look for the coming clouds. 'Watch and pray' the Lord Jesus said (Matthew 26:41), and when the apostle Paul urged the Ephesians to be praying at all seasons in the Spirit, he added 'and watching thereunto in all perseverance' (Ephesians 6:18). The Lord Jesus gave us a remarkable promise when He said 'all things, whatsoever ye shall ask in prayer, believing, ye shall receive' (Matthew 21:22). How can we pray that sort of believing prayer? Surely it requires that the Holy Spirit guide us into the mind of God on that particular matter. Elijah knew that it was God's will to send the rain, so he prayed in faith, looking confidently for the answer.

Linked with that is Elijah's persistence in prayer. He did not give up until the answer was received. Six times he prayed and each time the servant reported there was nothing. But he kept on praying. We 'ought always to pray, and not to faint'.

NINETY-NINE: HE IS ABLE

One morning by the sea of Galilee when seven of the apostles came back from their fishing trip, the Lord Jesus had prepared a cooked breakfast for them on the beach. And as He invited those tired men to eat, He served them. What wondrous grace: the Son of God Himself, raised and glorified and visiting them from heaven, and providing for them despite their waywardness. That was a demonstration of the love that 'Beareth all things, believeth all things, hopeth all things, endureth all things'. Love (agapē) never fails. It didn't in this case and it never will.

For our strong encouragement we remind ourselves that 'Jesus Christ is the same yesterday and today, yea and for ever' (Hebrews 13:8). The same gentle, tender Master sits today on heaven's throne and He cares for us as deeply as He did for those fishermen. The writer to the Hebrews highlights His present work upon the throne when he says ' we have not a high priest that cannot be touched with the feeling of our infirmities; but one that hath been in all points tempted like as we are, yet without sin' (Hebrews 4:15).

How thankful we are that He is there at His Father's side, understanding us so completely in all our frailty, and because 'he himself hath suffered being tempted, he is able to succour them that are tempted' (Hebrews 2:18).

'Able to succour' and 'able to save'. Putting those two great promises together faith has strong encouragement to draw near to God through Him. For the promise is that 'he is able to save to the uttermost them that draw near

unto God through him, seeing he ever liveth to make intercession for them'
(Hebrews 7:25). There is no experience in life in which He cannot help; no
depths to which we sink from which He cannot deliver us, if we come to God
through Him. So when Satan tempts us to despair let us send up our urgent
prayer to the throne of grace, and at the right time we shall receive the help
we so much need.

ONE HUNDRED: LOOKING UNTO JESUS

'What doest thou here, Elijah?' (1 Kings 19:9). Was God giving him an opportunity of confessing his failure and asking for forgiveness? It would have been well for Elijah if he had grasped it, but he didn't. He poured out the same complaint, 'I have been very jealous for the LORD, the God of hosts; for the children of Israel have forsaken thy covenant, thrown down thine altars, and slain thy prophets with the sword: and I, even I only, am left; and they seek my life, to take it away'. He was feeling very sorry for himself and that may well have been at the root of his trouble, thinking too much about himself. When we get our eyes off the Lord there is always that danger. 'Looking unto Jesus the author and perfecter of our faith' (Hebrews 12:2) is an exhortation we must never forget.

In Romans 11 the apostle Paul comments on this incident in Elijah's life: he quotes what he said to God, and the divine comment is 'he pleadeth with God against Israel'. That word gives us an insight into the prophet's mistake. It is one thing to confess the sin of one's people; many men of God have done that, but always with a view to their forgiveness and restoration. But in his deep discouragement Elijah prayed against them and that was a serious mistake. But let's get back to the cave and consider Elijah standing at its entrance as he quietened his heart and heard God speaking to him in that sound of gentle stillness. 'I have stilled and quieted my soul; like a weaned child with his mother' David said, and we need to do that, too. Only as we quieten our hearts shall we hear His voice. If we are full of anxieties and distractions it will be hard to hear God speaking to us.

ONE HUNDRED AND ONE: ELISHA ANOINTING ELIJAH

'Go, return on thy way' (1 Kings 19:15) was God's word to Elijah when he met him at the entrance of the cave. Elijah had made a mistake. He had run away without any instruction from God and he had to retrace his steps and go back the way he had come, as we have to do sometimes, when we make mistakes. One of his immediate tasks was to anoint young Elisha to be prophet in his place. God had another man ready, as He always has, and Elijah found him ploughing in the fields and himself guiding one of the yoke of oxen. This young man was not afraid of a day's hard work.

God had been speaking to Elisha's heart. He was calling him to His service and now the old prophet arrived with confirmation of the call he had been feeling so strongly. He understood the significance of Elijah throwing his cloak over his shoulders, and when Elijah turned as though to walk away, the young man ran after him. 'Let me, I pray thee, kiss my father and my mother, and then I will follow thee', he said. 'Go back again', Elijah replied, 'for what have I done to thee?' But that was said to prove him surely, to give him the opportunity of counting the cost. Elisha was equal to it. His mind was made up, his heart was set. Slaying his oxen and burning the ploughing equipment to make a fire to cook the meat, he gave it to the people with him and they ate together in a parting meal, and then he was on his way, following Elijah. He had made the break with family ties. There was nothing whatever to hold him back. It says 'he arose, and went after Elijah, and ministered unto him'. It was humble work to start with, but Elisha was content. 'Whosoever would become great among you, shall be your minister', the Lord Jesus said (Mark 10:43), and the younger man would count it an honour to wait upon God's prophet.

Elijah had been a unique man, one who had towered above his fellows. He had withstood onslaughts of evil as a rock shakes off the waves that beat upon it. He was one of the most dramatic figures in Israel's history. His name means 'My God is Jah' and his service for God had been characterized by fearless judgement. But his service was nearly over and the younger man stepping into his place was called to a gentler ministry. Elisha's name means 'My God is salvation' and in many ways his life reminds us of the Lord Jesus in His service. The mighty works Elisha did were mostly for healing and blessing, in contrast to Elijah who was so often called to acts of judgement on account of the people's sin.

ONE HUNDRED AND TWO: PASS IT ON

Paul's word to Timothy was, 'the things which thou hast heard from me among many witnesses, the same commit thou to faithful men, who shall be able to teach others also' (2 Timothy 2:2). God's truth must be passed on as each new generation rises. It was not just a question of the things Timothy heard Paul saying when he was in his company. It was definite systematic instruction, the older man passing on to the younger a precious deposit of divine truth which he was to treasure and guard and in turn pass on to others. Four generations are envisaged in this one verse, faithful men passing on divine truth as younger men rose to responsibility. And we notice the careful instruction, ' the things which thou hast heard from me ... the same commit thou to faithful men'. That is important. God's truth must be preserved and passed on in all its purity, nothing added to it and certainly nothing taken away.

We are living in days when we need to be specially watchful about this, for Satan is doing his utmost to undermine the confidence of believers in the Word of God. We must stand boldly for the truth of the inerrancy of Scripture, that every word of our Bible in the original languages was the inspired Word of God. We believe that 'Every scripture is inspired of God, and profitable for teaching, for reproof, for correction, for instruction which is in righteousness: that the man of God may be complete, furnished completely unto every good work' (2 Timothy 3:16,17 RVM). So let us treasure every part of it and grasp every opportunity of teaching it to others as diligently as we can.

ONE HUNDRED AND THREE: ELIJAH IN NABOTH'S VINEYARD

Elijah may well have wondered whether because of his failure he had forfeited the right to be used by God. But it was not so. Whatever regrets may have filled his heart in regard to his despondency when he sat under the juniper tree and asked to die, God was taking up His servant once again. It says 'the word of the LORD came to Elijah the Tishbite'. It was just like the old days when the Word of God came to him and he had to speak it out faithfully and fearlessly. Once again he was being sent with a message to king Ahab. 'Arise, go down to meet Ahab king of Israel, which dwelleth in Samaria: behold, he is in the vineyard of Naboth, whither he is gone down to take possession of it' (1 Kings 21:17,18).

Ahab had not changed despite the remarkable demonstration of God's power on mount Carmel and despite the fact that the prophets of Baal had been slain. He was still the same Ahab and his wicked queen was still scheming behind the scenes. In this case it had to do with Naboth's vineyard which adjoined the king's palace. Ahab wanted it badly and offered to do business with Naboth. He was prepared to give him a better vineyard or the value of it in money. But Naboth would not agree. It was his God-given inheritance handed down from his fathers, and he would not let it go. God had said it was to be passed down the family line, so as far as Naboth was concerned it was God's word versus the king's, and he was such a man that neither the king's reward nor the king's wrath would persuade him to go against the word of the Lord. Fearlessly he stood his ground. He explained it was the inheritance of his fathers and he could not, and must not give it up. All honour to him!

His courage and faithfulness stand on the page of Scripture as a great example to us, for we have an inheritance which God has given us and we are required to guard it with similar diligence. It is not the inheritance of which the apostle Peter writes which is incorruptible and undefiled and reserved in heaven for us. We cannot lose that inheritance. It belongs to all who have been born again. There is another inheritance of which the apostle Paul spoke to the elders of Ephesus, when he said, 'I commend you to God, and to the word of his grace, which is able to build you up, and to give you the inheritance among all them that are sanctified' (Acts 20:32).

ONE HUNDRED AND FOUR: WHERE IS THE GOD OF ELIJAH?

Jordan was the final place to which God sent Elijah and Elisha went with him. Elijah took his cloak and with it smote the waters of Jordan and they parted to allow the two prophets to go over on dry ground. Then the older man said, 'Ask what I shall do for thee, before I be taken from thee' (2 Kings 2:9), and it drew from Elisha that remarkable request, 'I pray thee, let a double portion of thy spirit be upon me'. Obviously he was very conscious of the great responsibility resting upon him and he knew he could only go forward by the enabling of the divine Spirit who had been so much in evidence in Elijah's life.

But Elijah said it was a hard thing that he had asked, for the fulness and power of the Holy Spirit is not something which God grants lightly. It calls for a holy life, devoted to God. There are conditions to be fulfilled and for Elisha the condition was 'if thou see me when I am taken from thee, it shall be so unto thee'. And he did! He allowed nothing to come between himself and Elijah, nothing that would obscure his vision of him. What a lesson for those of us who follow the Lord Jesus. The scripture says 'they two went on', 'they two stood by Jordan', 'they two went over' referring to Jordan, and then 'as they still went on, and talked, that, behold, there appeared a chariot of fire, and horses of fire, which parted them both asunder; and Elijah went up by a whirlwind into heaven.' So God's great servant was away home to glory, truly an abundant entrance into the eternal kingdom.

Elisha picked up Elijah's cloak which fell from him as he went. He knew it well. Had it not rested on his shoulders when God confirmed His call to him, when the old prophet anointed him with oil? Taking it up he stood by the Jordan river. 'Where is the LORD, the God of Elijah?' he cried. Where is He indeed? He is with His young servant and He proved it by parting the waters of Jordan to allow him to pass over. And the sons of the prophets saw it happen and they said, 'the spirit of Elijah doth rest on Elisha'.

ONE HUNDRED AND FIVE: ELIJAH ON THE MOUNT

The apostle Peter never forgot the experience he had, along with James and John, on the holy mount when the Lord Jesus was transfigured before them. 'we were eyewitnesses of his majesty', he said, 'for he received from God the Father honour and glory' (2 Peter 1:16,17). It was His inward glory, the glory of God, shining out from His human body. They had never seen Him like this before. His face shone like the sun and His garments became white as the light. God is light and He covers Himself with light like a garment, so when the Lord Jesus was revealed in power and glory He was enveloped by light that was brighter than the noon-day sun.

Moses and Elijah appeared, talking with the Lord Jesus, and they also were seen in glorious splendour: Moses the great law-giver and Elijah representing all the prophets. They spoke with Him about His departure which was soon to take place at Jerusalem. It was a subject they were both familiar with, for the law and the prophets had foretold that the Christ must suffer and die. As they spoke together the three disciples would be listening. What an experience for them. Peter said, 'Lord, it is good for us to be here' and so it was. Any fresh revelation of their Master was good for them, as it is also for us. It will affect our lives as it did theirs.

Then a cloud came and overshadowed them and they were afraid as they entered into it. They need not have been, for they were about to have one of the greatest experiences of their lives. God's presence was in the cloud, as it had been in the past. When He descended on Mount Sinai and gave Moses the law for His people, the mountain was covered with a thick, dark cloud. But this was a bright cloud, for we are 'not come unto a mount … that burned with fire, and unto blackness, and darkness, and tempest' (Hebrews 12:18). No, that belonged to the old covenant and to the giving of the law. We are no longer under that law; we are under grace and the voice out of the cloud brought the supreme message for our day of grace.

'This is my beloved Son, in whom I am well pleased; hear ye him' (Matthew 17:5). God had spoken the same commendation of His Son once before, at the river Jordan when the Lord Jesus was baptized by John, and now once again, the same important, timeless message, with these words added, 'hear ye him'. And when they looked up, they saw no one but Jesus only. Yes, that is the message of this mountain. Whatever other lessons we may learn, and there are plenty, this one stands supreme.

ONE HUNDRED AND SIX: BE NOT AFRAID

We live in days when the Word of God is being challenged, and when some are casting doubt upon the authority of the word of Christ. We need to hear again the divine command from the holy mount, for our acceptable service to God depends upon our obedience to it. And is it not interesting, and comforting, that the first words which fell from the lips of the Lord Jesus after the Father's stirring command were, 'Arise, and be not afraid' (Matthew 17:7)? They had been afraid, but now the experience of His glory has passed, and they see Him again as they have always known Him, the same gentle, caring Master, and He spoke peace to their hearts.

With their fears calmed they wended their way down the mountainside. How they would love to have stayed longer. Maybe that is why Peter proposed building three tabernacles. Did he think the Lord Jesus was going to introduce His glorious kingdom and take up His power and reign? Maybe, but that is not yet. The way to the throne was via the Cross, and down below human hearts were breaking and crying out for the help which He alone could give. So from the mountain they descended, but not alone. Moses and Elijah have gone, but the One whom they had glimpsed in His glory and power was with them still, in lowly form, still going about and ' doing good, and healing all that were oppressed of the devil; for God was with him' (Acts 10:38). As they listened to Him and gave Him the allegiance of their hearts, they had a part with Him in His ministry to those who were suffering because of sin. And so shall we.

One day we are going to see Him in His glory, and not just a passing glimpse, but lasting for ever. Until that glorious day it is our privilege to serve the One whom the Father has delighted to honour.

ONE HUNDRED AND SEVEN: THE POWER OF THE CROSS

'The word of the cross is to them that are perishing foolishness; but unto us which are being saved it is the power of God' (1 Corinthians 1:18). So wrote the apostle Paul as he defended his determination to preach no other message than Christ and Him crucified. Later he added the remarkable statement that 'the weakness of God is stronger than men' (1:25). The weakness of God! The words seem incongruous, but maybe we glimpse something of their meaning as we consider Simon of Cyrene being compelled to help God's Servant as He carried His Cross to Calvary. Christ the power of God, but in extreme physical weakness as He did battle with Satan's hosts. By the power of God he put off from Himself the principalities and powers, and made a show of them openly as He triumphed over them.

A dying Man, nailed to a Cross, how could He be God's way of salvation? To Jews it was 'a stumbling block, and unto Gentiles foolishness; but unto them that are called, both Jews and Greeks, Christ the power of God, and the wisdom of God' (1:23,24). In His infinite knowledge and wisdom God had decreed that 'apart from shedding of blood there is no remission' (Hebrews 9:22), and in those dark hours on Calvary He provided in the blood of His Son what heaven demanded and what men on earth so deeply needed. 'O the depth of the riches both of the wisdom and the knowledge of God! How unsearchable are his judgements, and his ways past tracing out' (Romans 11:33).

ONE HUNDRED AND EIGHT: KEEP YOURSELF PURE

A group of boys sat huddled around a hurricane lamp in a tent. It was the late-night talk at a Bible Camp and the camp leader was not pulling his punches. He had the knack of taking a verse or a phrase out of the Bible and making it hit home with hammer-force. Some of his talks will never be forgotten. I know, because I was one of the lads. The night I remember best he was speaking from these words which Paul wrote to Timothy: 'Do not be hasty in the laying on of hands, nor participate in another man's sins; keep yourself pure' (1 Timothy 5:22 RSV). Other people may sin, but that does not mean I can do the same. That is the point he was making. 'We are each responsible to God for our own behaviour' he said, 'and God says we are to keep ourselves pure'. But why? People do not place much importance on moral purity these days. Anything goes in the world. True, but Christians do not belong to the world - they belong to the Lord Jesus Christ. God says '... as he who called you is holy, be holy yourselves in all your conduct' (1 Peter 1:15 RSV). 'Holy' is from the same root as the word 'pure' and really means separated, or set apart, for God. That makes us different, of course, from other people who do not belong to Him, and we must be prepared for that. God is our Father, and because He is holy He expects us to be too; and notice, it says 'in all your conduct', so that covers every part of our lives.

ONE HUNDRED AND NINE: FAITH TO CONQUER

The first time we read of Caleb is in Numbers 13 when he was chosen as one of the princes to spy out the land. He represented his tribe, Judah. He was a prince by nature as well as by rank; a princely man of faith. Like his ten brethren, he also saw the great stature of the people of the land and their fenced cities. He saw the giants too. But he saw beyond, for faith always takes a long distance view. He saw the Lord who had promised to give them the land and was waiting to fulfil His promise.

'If the LORD delight in us, then he will bring us into this land, and give it unto us' (Numbers 14:8). That was the 'if' of argument, not of doubt. There was no question that the Lord delighted in them. Had He not delivered them from the tyranny of Egypt, divided the Red Sea, fed them with daily manna and provided a pillar of fire and cloud to guide them by night and day? The whole matter was as clear as daylight to Caleb's faith and he stood courageously by his convictions, even at the risk of being stoned. 'Trust ye in the LORD for ever: for in the LORD JEHOVAH is an everlasting rock' (Isaiah 26:4). This man of faith stood firm as a rock!

'They that wait upon the LORD shall renew their strength'. That was the secret of Caleb's strength. 'They shall mount up with wings as eagles' and so he did, at Kadesh-barnea and again at Hebron. Faith soared high on those occasions. But what of those thirty-eight long years in the waste and howling wilderness?

Surely those years were an even greater test of his faith. They were. But 'they that wait upon the LORD ... shall run, and not be weary; they shall walk, and not faint'. Caleb proved the truth of that word. Shall we not be encouraged by his faith and ask the Lord's help to do the same?

ONE HUNDRED AND TEN: FAITHFUL AMIDST UNFAITHFULNESS

It must have been a bewildering time for the godly Israelite when the kingdom was divided, with ten tribes following Jeroboam, while Judah and Benjamin maintained their allegiance to David's grandson, Rehoboam. From the outset it was evident that king Jeroboam had no intention of following the way of the Lord. Intent on personal gain, he was actuated by human cleverness rather than faith. At the beginning of his reign he made two golden calves, setting up one in Bethel and the other in Dan, thus introducing a spurious worship which God referred to as 'his sin wherewith he made Israel to sin' (1 Kings 15:34). Time and again that condemnation occurs in Old Testament history. The seriousness of what he did could hardly he exaggerated. There was no place in his new system for the priests and the Levites, and it says 'Jeroboam and his sons cast them off, that they should not execute the priest's office unto the LORD' (2 Chronicles 11:14). So they left their suburbs and their possessions and came to Jerusalem where they could continue their God-given service in His house. Their example inspired many of the godly in the northern kingdom of Israel to do the same, and verse 16 of the same chapter makes stirring reading.

'And after them, out of all the tribes of Israel, such as set their hearts to seek the LORD, the God of Israel, came to Jerusalem to sacrifice unto the LORD, the God of their fathers.' They uprooted themselves and relocated in Jerusalem so that they could sacrifice to the Lord. Why? Because Jerusalem was the place where God had put His name. His Temple was there and the service of God associated with it. His clear word through Moses had never been repealed: '... unto the place which the LORD your God shall choose out of all your tribes to put his name there, even unto his habitation shall ye seek, and thither thou shalt come: and thither ye shall bring your burnt offerings, and your sacrifices, and your tithes' (Deuteronomy 12:5,6).

All that was precious in their national life was centred in Jerusalem, the city of the great King. These worthy souls acknowledged that and they set their hearts to seek the Lord. Cost what it may they determined to obey His Word. It was costly. Great sacrifice was involved. But God had spoken and His Word had to be obeyed. God records their faithfulness and adds the comment that they strengthened the kingdom of Judah and made king Rehoboam strong. Such people would strengthen any movement. They had deep convictions, rooted in God's Word, and by these convictions they ordered their lives.

ONE HUNDRED AND ELEVEN: SITTING AT HIS FEET

Mary of Bethany made a wise choice. She 'also sat at the Lord's feet, and heard his word' (Luke 10:39). 'Also' may indicate that she had already helped in the preparation of the meal, and then while her sister Martha became distracted she quietened her heart to listen to what the Master had to share with her. The Lord Jesus commended her. 'Mary hath chosen the good part', He said. So before their divine Guest and His apostles enjoyed the hospitality of this well-loved home, He spread a table for Mary and she supped with Him, in fulfilment of His word in Revelation 3:20. Rich things He had to share. Of that we can be sure.

Mary received the good part which would never be taken away from her. We must make our choice also, for the Lord knocks at the heart's door of each of His own, longing for communion, to share with us His love and joy and peace. 'Let me see thy countenance, let me hear thy voice' (Song of Songs 2:14). What a wonder! He wants to hear our voice; but first we must hear His voice and open the door to the secret place of our hearts. Then He will share with us and we with Him. That is communion.

The Tamils of south India have a word for 'disciple' which means 'one who sits at the feet'. It implies submission and a willingness to listen. Mary took that place. Did she sit alone? The Gospel record suggests so. Was she the only one who wasn't too busy that day? We do not know, but we do know that the Master was very willing to spend time with one individual, if there was a willingness to sit and listen. Each one of us is precious to Him. 'if any man hear my voice'. He waits only to be welcomed in, and He will enjoy what we have for Him, and then we shall share with Him what He has for us.

ONE HUNDRED AND TWELVE: TO GAIN CHRIST

It was in Caesarea Philippi at the foot of mount Hermon, where the river Jordan finds one of its sources, that the Lord Jesus began 'to shew unto his disciples, how that he must ... suffer ... and be killed, and the third day be raised up' (Matthew 16:21). In Peter's rebuke He recognized the voice of Satan attempting to deter him from fulfilling what Peter later understood and declared to be 'the determinate counsel ... of God' (Acts 2:23). In His reply the Master said 'thou mindest not the things of God, but the things of men'.

They stand in stark contrast. The things of God lead through suffering and death to resurrection and life. The Lord Jesus was on His way to Calvary and He invited His disciples, and us, to follow Him; adding the wonderful promise that 'whosoever would save his life shall lose it: and whosoever shall lose his life for my sake shall find it' (Matthew 16:25).

So it is a question of gain and loss viewed from two different perspectives. The things of men may be attractive as they were to Eve when tempted in the garden, but they are temporal and end in eternal loss. In the things of God the eye of faith discerns eternal gain. Moses is an outstanding example of a man who got the long distance view, 'Accounting the reproach of Christ greater riches than the treasures of Egypt: for he looked unto the recompense of reward' (Hebrews 11:26). The apostle Paul counted all earthly gains as loss that he might gain Christ.

ONE HUNDRED AND THIRTEEN: ABIDING WITH CHRIST

'Rabbi ... where abidest thou?' asked Andrew and John. 'Come, and ye shall see' was the reply. 'and they abode with him that day' (John 1:38,39). Those two disciples got a taste of fellowship with the Son of God that memorable day which greatly influenced the whole of their lives. Soon afterwards they left their homes and fishing to follow Him, and companying with the Lord Jesus became a daily experience. Nor did it end when He returned to heaven, for aged John wrote 'our fellowship is with the Father, and with his Son Jesus Christ' (1 John 1:3).

Appropriately John was the one chosen by God to reveal to us this great truth of fellowship (Greek koinōnia - sharing in common) with the Persons of the Godhead. The great truth is that the Father and the Son want to share with us the things which They enjoy together. What a wonder! As we pursue our mundane tasks of daily life our minds can be occupied with the very thoughts which occupy the divine mind. The Father and the Son sincerely desire to share with us.

The Lord Jesus enlarges on this glorious truth in John 14:21,23. Notice the promises, 'we will come ... and make our abode with him', and 'I will manifest myself unto him'. Notice also the conditions, 'He that hath my commandments, and keepeth them, he it is that loveth me', and 'If a man love me, he will keep my word'. The whole experience is based in love. Six times agapē love is mentioned in these two verses. It is love which issues in obedience and that in turn results in communion. So the sequence is, love, obedience, communion, joy, for John adds 'these things we write, that your joy may be fulfilled' (1 John 1:4 RVM).

This is the secret of the believer's joy. The Lord Jesus emphasizes it again in John 15:10,11 and once again the four-fold sequence is spelt out for us. 'If ye keep my commandments, ye shall abide in my love' and what is that but communion? 'These things have I spoken unto you, that my joy may be in you, and that your joy may be fulfilled'. My commandments, My love, My joy. God grant that His words may sink deep into our hearts until His joy becomes the hallmark of our lives.

ONE HUNDRED AND FOURTEEN: BURNING HEARTS

'He made as though he would go further' (Luke 24:28). It was not that the Lord Jesus did not wish to join these two disciples at their evening meal. He did, very much so. But He was waiting for an invitation. Once invited He was quick to respond. 'He went in to abide with them'. 'I will come in to him, and will sup with him, and he with me' is the glorious promise of Revelation 3:20. He will share with us what we have for Him (however poor it be) and then welcome us to share what He has for us. That is communion, sharing together. And we need it deeply, do we not?

> Not a brief glance I beg, a passing word;
> But as Thou dwelt'st with Thy disciples, Lord,
> Familiar, condescending, patient, free,
> Come not to sojourn, but abide with me!
> (H.F.Lyte)

But why did the Master vanish out of their sight as soon as they recognized Him? Because He had to teach them that though they had known Him after the flesh, yet now they would know Him so no more (see 2 Corinthians 5:16). That is why on that memorable journey to Emmaus He interpreted to them in all the Scriptures the things concerning Himself. In future they would find Him in the Scriptures. It was an important lesson He had come to teach them, so important that He spoke similarly to His apostles who were met together in the Upper Room that same night. 'These are my words which I spake unto you, while I was yet with you ... which are written in the law of Moses, and the prophets, and the psalms, concerning me. Then opened he their mind, that they might understand the scriptures' (Luke 24:44,45).

This is the era of the Holy Spirit who has come to make the things of Christ real and precious to us. 'He shall glorify me: for he shall take of mine, and shall declare it unto you' (John 16:14) the Master promised as He told them about the other Comforter whom the Father would send in His Name. But the Holy Spirit can only do that if we take time with our Bibles, not only to read but to meditate and to ponder. Then He will do His gracious work and make our risen Lord and Master as real and as precious to us as He was to His disciples in the days of His flesh. And the fire will kindle until we also have burning hearts.

ONE HUNDRED AND FIFTEEN: 'THIS IS MY BELOVED', AND THIS IS MY FRIEND

The disciples in Laodicea were lukewarm. Like the saints in Ephesus they had left their first love. Materialism lay at the root of their problem. We are 'rich, and have gotten riches' they said. Nothing wrong with that, provided the riches had been honestly gained. But the next statement revealed their terrible mistake, 'and have need of nothing' (Revelation 3:17). What a fearful thing for any disciple of the Lord Jesus to say. Consequently, He was outside of their lives as far as communion was concerned. So with pierced hand He stood knocking at their heart's door. 'If any man hear my voice and open the door, I will come in to him'. The voice and the knock! 'It is the voice of my beloved that knocketh, saying, Open to me' (Song of Songs 5:2). 'My beloved put in his hand by the hole of the door, and my heart was moved for him' (v.4).

Do we sometimes make the same mistake and find ourselves living more in the atmosphere of Ecclesiastes with all its things, rather than in the Song of Songs with Him whom our souls love? For we do love Him. Of course we do! and when we hear His voice and respond to it, His word is 'No longer do I call you servants; for the servant knoweth not what his lord doeth: but I have called you friends; for all things that I heard from my Father I have made known unto you' (John 15:15). What a wonderful promise! All things, Lord? Yes, all things that I heard from My Father. And lest some should argue that that was a promise made specifically to His apostles look at chapter 16, where the Lord Jesus is speaking of the time when ' the Spirit of truth, is come' (v.13), and that most certainly applies to us.

'He shall glorify me: for he shall take of mine, and shall declare it unto you. All things whatsoever the Father hath are mine: therefore said I, that he taketh of mine, and shall declare it unto you' (John 16:14,15). All things that belong to the Father belong equally to the Son and these things the Holy Spirit makes known to us. 'the communion of the Holy Ghost' the apostle Paul calls it (2 Corinthians 13:14; Philippians 2:1). Part of His work in our hearts is to make this communion possible and real. Ponder the truth of it. Let us turn it over in our minds until the absolute wonder of it grips our hearts. All things! 'He that spared not his own Son, but delivered him up for us all, how shall he not also with him freely give us all things?' (Romans 8:32). 'all things are yours ... and ye are Christ's; and Christ is God's' (1 Corinthians 3:21,23).

ONE HUNDRED AND SIXTEEN: YEARNING LOVE

Hosea is a story of divine love set against the background of tragedy in the prophet's domestic life; a story of an unfaithful wife, a broken home and a broken heart, but of love triumphing in the end. It is doubtful if Hosea could have brought God's message to His people with the same pathos and appeal had he not passed through such a bitter experience himself. God and His prophet both suffered the pain and sadness caused by unfaithfulness; both experienced the bitterness of wounded love.

Hosea has been called the prophet of love. In his prophecy we get a glimpse into the very heart of God. 'When Israel was a child, then I loved him' (Hosea 11:1). God was harking back to the beginning days when He called His son out of Egypt. 'I taught Ephraim to go' (Hosea 11:3). It is nursery language, of a father teaching his little son to walk. 'I took them on my arms', strong father arms supporting, upholding. 'I drew them with cords of a man, with bands of love' (Hosea 11:4). I loved … and called … I taught … I took … I healed … I drew them. God did it all, in the love of His heart.

Love was reciprocated in those days. 'I remember for thee the kindness of thy youth, the love of thine espousals' (Jeremiah 2:2). But they had long since forgotten God and left their first love; but He had not forgotten them. 'O Ephraim, what shall I do unto thee?' (Hosea 6:4). He pleaded with them, but their hearts were deaf to His entreaties. 'I will go and return to my place, till they acknowledge their offence, and seek my face' (Hosea 5:15). Days of affliction followed, inevitably 'For whom the Lord loveth he chasteneth' (Hebrews 12:6). But only 'till they acknowledge their offence'. There is always an 'until', for chastening is calculated to yield peaceable fruit of righteousness. Through chastening days His love pursued them still.

'Love never faileth.' 'How shall I give thee up, Ephraim?' It was the cry of God's Father heart. There was no reason in justice why they should not be given up, but there was a reason in love. 'mine heart is turned within me, my compassions are kindled together' (Hosea 11:8). 'Kindled together' is one word in Hebrew. When Joseph caught sight of his own brother Benjamin he could not contain himself. He left the room and wept, for 'his bowels did yearn upon his brother' (Genesis 43:30). 'Yearn' translates the same Hebrew word rendered 'kindled together' in Hosea 11:8. The same word again. 'My compassions are yearning' God says.

ONE HUNDRED AND SEVENTEEN: TWO WAYS OF FOLLOWING

'And Jesus arose, and followed him, and so did his disciples' (Matthew 9:19). It is an arresting word; it comes in the story of Jairus, whose little daughter was dying, and he came pleading for help. The scripture says, '... Jesus arose, and followed him'. It is what we would expect, and yet, it is not the usual way, is it? We are far more familiar with men rising up and following Jesus. He is the Master, and in His all-authority He called, 'Come, follow me'. Time and again, the gospel records provide the stirring accounts of men who heard the call, and saying goodbye to home and friends, rose up and followed Him.

But here, the order is reversed, and Jesus rose up and followed Jairus. In an agony of heart, he came pleading for help, and his request did not fall on deaf ears. The Master's response was immediate and unhesitating. He arose and followed him. It was divine love following hard after human need. Where there are broken hearts, men and women hopeless and helpless, our compassionate Master is never far away. He is there, following, pursuing with a love that never fails, that suffers long and is kind.

The kind of joy He brings is seen in that little family that day as He handed back their little girl, alive from the dead. In His thoughtfulness, He reminded them to give her something to eat. Divine love forgets nothing, not even the tiny details of life. '... Jesus arose, and followed him, and so did his disciples'. And therein lies a message for us! If we are true followers of this compassionate

Master, we also shall need to follow wherever human hearts are crying out for help. And so they are, all around us! This article was written in India, where human need cries out so pathetically and so urgently. But, is it not so in every land, if only our hearts are tuned to hear, and our eyes anointed to see? The hungry and hopeless and helpless, lost in a maze of sin and hurrying to a lost eternity, are not they calling out for our help? And, the Master we follow is calling from heaven's throne and urging us to follow where He has led the way.

ONE HUNDRED AND EIGHTEEN: 'TO WHOM WILL YOU LIKEN ME?'

That was God's question to Israel. 'To whom will ye liken me, and make me equal, and compare me, that we may be like?' (Isaiah 46:5). And there follows in fine poetic imagery the striking contrast between the gods of Babylon, or any other false gods, and the living and true God. The former are made by men and what they make they must bear as a burden, carrying them from one place to another. In wonderful contrast we are made by the living God and what He makes He carries. The promise is 'even to old age I am he, and even to hoar hairs will I carry you: I have made, and I will bear; yea, I will carry, and will deliver' (Isaiah 46:4). And then follows the pertinent question, 'To whom will ye liken me?'

A god of gold or silver, 'one shall cry unto him, yet can he not answer, nor save him out of his trouble' (v.7). But the living God who is 'our refuge and strength' is 'a very present help in trouble' (Psalm 46:1). 'call upon me in the day of trouble' God says, 'I will deliver thee, and thou shalt glorify me' (Psalm 50:15), and that promise has never been known to fail! As our minds travel from one great blessing to another we give thanks that like the Thessalonians we have 'turned unto God from idols, to serve a living and true God, and to wait for his Son from heaven' (1 Thessalonians 1:9,10).

ONE HUNDRED AND NINETEEN: GUARD YOURSELF FROM IDOLS

Is there any comparison between the idols Israel cherished in their hearts (see Ezekiel 20:16) and the idols from which aged John pleaded with his spiritual children to guard themselves (1 John 5:21)? Yes, there is indeed, for the word 'idol' literally means 'that which is seen' and it refers not only to that which captivates the physical sight, but also to anything the evil one may use to obscure our spiritual vision, to distract us from looking off unto Jesus, the Author and Perfecter of faith. So easily other things or persons can work their way into our hearts' affections, but examined in the light of eternity are they not vain things (see Acts 14:15) and things of nought (see 1 Corinthians 8:4)? If they succeed in winning the place in our hearts that belongs to our Master and Lord we shall find ourselves carrying burdens which will weigh us down in the spiritual race. How important therefore to heed the apostle John's final appeal, 'My little children, guard yourselves from idols' (1 John 5:21).

ONE HUNDRED AND TWENTY: MUTUAL SATISFACTION

'As for me, I shall behold thy face in righteousness: I shall be satisfied, when I awake, with thy likeness' (Psalm 17:15). So wrote King David as he contrasted his satisfaction with that of men of the world, whose portion is in this life. That was the vital difference between them, for there was a spiritual dimension in David's life. The Lord was his portion. 'They are satisfied with children', he wrote. So was David, of course. There is ample evidence in the Scriptures of his deep love for his family. But for the man of God there is more, much more. I shall be fully satisfied - for there is the thought of fulness in the Hebrew word - when I awake with Thy likeness.

This is one of the comparatively few Old Testament scriptures that refer plainly to resurrection. We know so much more about the subject than Old Testament saints did; but even so 'it is not yet made manifest what we shall be'. However, this we know, 'if he shall be manifested, we shall be like him; for we shall see him even as he is' (1 John 3:2). Glorious prospect! To see Him will be to be like Him. 'I shall behold thy face in righteousness'. To see the Lord's face is the ultimate in blessing. It was so for Israel.

'The LORD bless thee, and keep thee: the LORD make his face to shine upon thee, and be gracious unto thee: the LORD lift up his countenance upon thee, and give thee peace' was the blessing God commanded Aaron and his sons to bestow upon His people (Numbers 6:24-26). There could be nothing sweeter or more precious than that. 'His servants shall do him service; and they shall see his face' (Revelation 22:3,4) is one of the lovely promises with which God draws His Word to a close. And when we see Him we shall be like Him. Then, and only then, shall we be fully satisfied.

Isn't it wonderful when turning to Isaiah 53 to be reminded that the Lord Jesus also is not yet completely satisfied, for the prophet says, 'He shall see of the travail of his soul, and shall be satisfied' (verse 11)? God's righteous Servant has justified many by bearing their iniquities, and only when all His justified ones are gathered home will His joy and satisfaction be complete. Then we shall behold His glory (see John 17:24) and He in turn will be glorified in His saints (see 2 Thessalonians 1:10). What a glorious contemplation!

ONE HUNDRED AND TWENTY-ONE: RISING UP EARLY

Eleven times God uses this expression about Himself in the writings of Jeremiah: '... rising up early and speaking' (7:13); '... my servants the prophets, daily rising up early and sending them' (7:25); '... rising up early and teaching them' (32:33). It is a figure of speech, of course, for 'he that keepeth Israel shall neither slumber nor sleep' (Psalm 121:4). Graciously God uses language familiar to us to express His earnestness and the depth of His desire for our well-being. In Jeremiah's day Israel refused to listen. In this they are presented to us as a solemn warning. By a simple transition of thought the expression God uses carries its message to our hearts, for the Scriptures record examples of those who rose early in their eagerness to commune with their God. David comes readily to mind. 'O LORD, in the morning shalt thou hear my voice; in the morning will I order my prayer unto thee, and will keep watch' (Psalm 5:3). The sons of Korah similarly '... in the morning shall my prayer come before thee' (Psalm 88:13).

Our prime Example is our blessed Master Himself, of course. Of Him Mark records 'in the morning, a great while before day, he rose up and went out, and departed into a desert place, and there prayed' (1:35). From Isaiah we learn that it was His daily habit: '... he wakeneth morning by morning, he wakeneth mine ear to hear as they that are taught' (50:4). It is a well-worn subject, constantly referred to, the importance of the Quiet Time, as it is sometimes called, but experience proves that we cannot too frequently remind one another of the absolute necessity of it, if a healthy spiritual life is to be maintained. It is possibly the first thing in our lives that our Adversary challenges. He knows, perhaps even better than we do, that if he can succeed in making us careless about our daily communion with the Lord, he has gained a resounding victory.

ONE HUNDRED AND TWENTY-TWO: PROMINENT AND UNNAMED MESSENGERS

Certain names stand out prominently as those who were mightily used in carrying the glorious message: Peter, Stephen, and then Paul and his companions. But for the most part the good news was carried by unnamed disciples: 'They therefore that were scattered abroad went about preaching the word' (Acts 8:4). Evangelize is the word in the Greek original. It means they carried the good tidings. Not to large crowds necessarily but to ones and twos whom they met along life's way. In Acts 11 we read of further persecution, and once again the same happy result that the Word was spread further afield. The more they were scattered, the more they spoke. Their Master's last words rang in their ears, and wherever they went they spoke of Him. 'Witness' is a legal word, used of a person who knows something, and tells what he knows. And we know something. Indeed we do! '... We know that the Son of God is come' (1 John 5:20). We know whom we have believed. But are we telling what we know? That is what turns believers into witnesses.

Witnesses! Martus is the word in the Greek, from which comes our English word 'martyr' one who bears witness by his death. And some of them did, too. 'They were stoned, they were sawn asunder, they were tempted, they were slain with the sword' (Hebrews 11:37). Noble men and women! A great cloud of witnesses indeed! And now it is our turn! Our authority comes from the risen Christ Himself; the power from the descended Holy Spirit, '... ye shall receive power ... and ye shall be my witnesses' (Acts 1:8). What a privilege! May the Lord touch our hearts, and touch our tongues, so that never a day passes without our speaking of Him.

ONE HUNDRED AND TWENTY-THREE: THE STRANGER ON THE BEACH

'It is the Lord', John exclaimed joyfully as he grappled with the multitude of fishes swarming into the net. It dawned on him like a flash. The Stranger on the beach was their Lord and Master. Who else could it be with such obvious dominion over the fish of the sea? Did he perhaps recall the words of Psalm 8? He 'manifested himself ... on this wise' he wrote later in his gospel record (21:1).

But that was not the only manifestation on that memorable morning. Seven tired and hungry men found breakfast cooked and ready for them when they dragged their boat to shore. As they warmed themselves around the fire their resurrected Master moved from one to another, serving them first with bread and then with the fish. What a wonderful manifestation of His love and care! The Lord of glory, from heaven's throne, come down to meet them and to share with them, giving them yet another example (could they ever forget how He had washed their feet?) of what it means in practical terms, when the scripture says 'through love be servants one to another' (Galatians 5:13).

'Bring of the fish which ye have now taken', He said, not because His supply was insufficient surely. That could never be. But in the spirit of Revelation 3:20, I suggest, 'if any man hear my voice and open the door, I will come in to him, and will sup with him, and he with me'. He wanted to share what they provided, as well as sharing with them His provision. What wonderful grace!

That is what fellowship is all about, it is sharing together. Reminding us that around that fire they would commune together. It surely would not be a silent meal. The Master had something to say specially to Simon Peter, we know, but Thomas and Nathanael and James and John would each carry away some of His words deep in their hearts.

ONE HUNDRED AND TWENTY-FOUR: BURNING HEARTS AND READY TONGUES

'Was not our heart burning within us, while he spake to us in the way, while he opened to us the scriptures?' (Luke 24:32).

Burning hearts

Thus did the two disciples describe their heart after the memorable walk with the Master. They had been talking of Him, and as they did so He drew near and went with them. As 'he interpreted to them in all the scriptures the things concerning himself' their hearts warmed until they could be described by only one word—burning hearts. How much we need hearts like these! The world is a cold place, cold with hatred, bitterness and sin, and sometimes it casts its chilling influence upon the child of God. How are we to keep our hearts warm? David said, 'While I was musing the fire kindled' (Psalm 39:3). They were 'the things concerning himself' which kindled the fire in the disciples' hearts, so it ever is. Occupation with Christ brings a glow to the heart which others will feel beside ourselves. What is there so warming as the love of Christ?

Opened eyes

Burning hearts and opened eyes! They go together. As long as their hearts were unbelieving their eyes were holden. But as they warmed to His words, their eyes were opened and they knew Him.

Running feet

Burning hearts and running feet! They could not wait until morning. Seven miles back they went that very night. Love lent speed to their feet. Weariness was forgotten for the joy that burned in their hearts.

Ready tongues

Burning hearts and ready tongues! Glad tidings of good things. Good indeed! Never a message as glad as this. What they had to tell served to confirm what the apostles were saying, 'The Lord is risen indeed and they rehearsed the things that happened in the way'. It was out of their own experience. Burning hearts must witness 'we cannot but speak the things which we saw and heard' said Peter and John (Acts 4:20).

Eyes to see, feet to run, tongues to tell – and they all issue from the burning heart. It is all too easy when the heart is aglow with love to Christ. 'Keep thy heart with all diligence; for out of it are the issues of life' (Proverbs 4:23). The issues not only of our lives, but, serious thought, also the lives of our neighbours.

ONE HUNDRED AND TWENTY-FIVE: AWAITING GOD

Abraham stands out as a great example to be followed. One of the outstanding characteristics of his life was his intercession. The scene in Gen.18 is set in Hebron, meaning 'fellowship'. Mamre means 'vision' or 'seeing', and by Mamre's oaks Abraham saw the Lord in very truth. After accepting his hospitality (precious foreshadowing surely of the promise of Rev.3:20), the divine Visitor stayed to commune with His servant. 'Shall I hide from Abraham that which I do?' He said. Truly 'The secret of the LORD is with them that fear him' (Ps.25:14). Abraham was taken into God's counsels that day, and his soul was stirred within him. 'And Abraham drew near'. So says the divine record. 'Draw nigh to God, and he will draw nigh to you' (Jas.4:8) is the promise of grace, and Abraham proved it true. 'Abraham stood yet before the LORD'. He would not easily give up. Humbly 'which am but dust and ashes', reverently 'Behold now, I have taken upon me to speak unto the Lord' and intelligently '... shall not the Judge of all the earth do right?' he pleaded with God. From 50 to 45 to 40. Then for 30 and 20, and still he stood before the Lord. 'Oh let not the Lord be angry, and I will speak yet but this once: peradventure ten shall be found there'. And God said, 'I will not destroy it for the ten's sake'. Great intercessor! We are challenged by his example. We 'ought always to pray, and not to faint' (Lk.18:1). God's judgement day is fast approaching and men are perishing in hopeless sin. And shall we not intercede? Surely it shall not be today among God's people as in Isaiah's day, when the Lord 'saw that there was no man, and wondered that there was no intercessor' (Is.59:16).

ONE HUNDRED AND TWENTY-SIX: 'I AM'

The Lord Jesus said, 'Before Abraham was, I am' (John 8:58). He loved to use that title during His sojourn on earth, linking it as He did with various aspects of human need, 'I am the bread of life', 'I am the light of the world', for example. It reminds us that our ever-present God and Saviour is the eternal I AM. We follow the precious truth a step further, for who has not been comforted by the great promise of Isaiah 41:10, 'Fear thou not, for I am with thee; be not dismayed, for I am thy God'? That Old Covenant promise is carried into our New Covenant experience by our risen Master's declaration, '... lo, I am with you alway, even unto the end of the world' (Matthew 28:20). 'I am with you'. Great words, great truth, linking His almighty power with our frailty and weakness.

Men and women of faith in all ages have grasped its significance and resting in it have been overcomers. To Jeremiah, trembling at the immensity of the task God was laying upon him, came the word, 'Be not afraid ... for I am with thee to deliver thee' (Jeremiah 1:8). The apostle Paul likewise in the night vision at Corinth heard the Voice saying, 'Be not afraid, but speak, and hold not thy peace: for I am with thee' (Acts 18:9,10). It banishes fear. It must do, for if He is with us, and for us, who can be against us? May God help each one of us to live in the peace and enjoyment of it.

ONE HUNDRED AND TWENTY-SEVEN: 'THE GOSPEL BEARING FRUIT AND INCREASING' (COLOSSIANS 1:5,6)

In the 20th century, world population increased by a staggering 4536 million. According to Whitaker's Almanack, it was estimated in 1900 at 1622 million and by the turn of the century demographers calculate that the figure had exceeded 6 billion. Every one of those millions of people is part of the world which God so loved, and still loves, that He gave His only-begotten Son for their salvation; every one of them a precious soul for whom Christ died. They were in God's mind before the foundation of the world, when 'According to the eternal purpose which he purposed in Christ Jesus our Lord' the elect among them were 'foreordained … unto adoption as sons through Jesus Christ unto himself' (Ephesians 3:11, 1:5). Glorious truth! We live to see God's eternal purpose being fulfilled and, by His grace, to have the privilege of a little part in the outworking of it.

'All souls are mine', God says, individually known and loved by Him, and each one with a right to hear of the Saviour who died. Clearly that fact was implied when God said of His Servant-Son, 'I will also give thee for a light to the Gentiles, that thou mayest be my salvation unto the end of the earth' (Isaiah 49:6). The same thought was surely in the Saviour's mind also when He commissioned His disciples to 'Go … into all the world, and preach the gospel to the whole creation' (Mark 16:15).

ONE HUNDRED AND TWENTY-EIGHT: PREACHING EVERYWHERE

'And they departed, and went throughout the villages, preaching the gospel, and healing everywhere' (Lk.9:6). The Master Himself had sent these apostles. He had given them the message and the power to speak it, and it remained only for them to go and preach it. This they did. To every village they went. Farther, and yet farther - until the precious message had been told in every place. A great work was begun that day, and the results of which will be seen only when we reach glory. To a similar noble work the apostle Paul devoted his life. 'the gospel which I preached unto you', he says in 1 Cor.15:1. To the Galatians he writes of 'the gospel which was preached by me' (1:11). Nor had his labours been confined to these parts only, for 'from Jerusalem, and round about even until Illyricum' he had 'fully preached the gospel of Christ' (Rom.15:19). What a preacher he was! Carrying the message of the Lord Jesus had been the burden of his life, and when his days of preaching were almost done, he urges his child Timothy to carry on the work. Very touching are his words when we remember they were written from prison, 'I charge thee in the sight of God, and of Christ Jesus ... preach the word ... do the work of an evangelist' (2 Tim.4:1,2,5). Down through the centuries men of God have taken up this message and carried it out. Love of the One whom they preached has urged them on and His power has upheld them. Thank God the same message is ours to preach today. The need is as urgent now as ever it was - perhaps more so, for His coming seems so near. Surely the very groan of men around us is a challenge to our hearts to speak to them of Jesus.

ONE HUNDRED AND TWENTY-NINE: THE HOLY ONE OF ISRAEL

This is one of God's titles used almost exclusively by Isaiah, and elsewhere only a few times in the Psalms and twice in Jeremiah. Isaiah understood, perhaps better than anyone else in his day, the truth conveyed in this title, for the life-changing vision he had in the year king Uzziah died, of the Lord sitting upon a throne, had impressed upon him for all time a deep sense of the intense holiness of God.

'Holy, holy, holy is the LORD of hosts ... the foundations of the thresholds were moved at the voice of him that cried', and Isaiah was moved, too, deeply moved. 'Woe is me!' he cried, 'for I am undone ... for mine eyes have seen the King, the LORD of hosts' (6:3–5 RV).

'What was conveyed to Isaiah by what he saw and heard?' asks James Packer in his book on Holiness. If you look up holy in a dictionary of theology, you will find that in both Testaments it is a word that applies primarily to God and expresses everything that sets him apart from us, making him different; everything that sets him above us, making him worshipful and awesome; and everything that sets him against us, making him an object of actual terror. The basic thought that the word carries is of God's separateness from us and of the contrast between what he is and what we are. If you think of holiness as a circle embracing everything about God that is different from what we are, the centre of the circle is God's moral and spiritual purity, which contrasts painfully with our twisted sinfulness. It was just this contrast that Isaiah perceived.

With such a vision burning in his heart Isaiah set himself to the task of calling the people back to their God. At the commencement of their nationhood the Holy One of Israel had decreed '… I am the LORD your God. You shall therefore consecrate yourselves, and you shall be holy; for I am holy' (Leviticus 11:44). Three times similar words are repeated in the book of Leviticus. But the people of Judah refused to obey and God clearly stated the reason '… they have rejected the law of the LORD of hosts, and despised the word of the Holy One of Israel' (Isaiah 5:24).

ONE HUNDRED AND THIRTY: I AM THE LORD

The Holy One of Israel proclaimed Himself to be a God full of compassion and gracious (Exodus 34:6 RV). His compassion was just one of the distinctive features of His holiness. It was evidenced in His law '... you shall not wholly reap the corners of your field ... nor shall you gather every grape of your vineyard; you shall leave them for the poor and the stranger: I am the LORD your God' (Leviticus 19:9,10 NKJV). That phrase 'I am the LORD' runs like a refrain through God's instructions, occurring 16 times in this chapter alone, for every commandment is set in relation to this fact. God's people must bear the character of their God. But Judah despised His word and their oppression of the poor was notorious, just one of the many evils God held against them '... the plunder of the poor is in your houses. What do you mean by crushing My people and grinding the faces of the poor?' (Isaiah 3:14,15).

Notice the expression 'My people' and sense the yearning love that He had for them. They were His people, His special treasure above all other nations of the world. They were constituted so when their forefathers pledged their obedience to God's word and He declared '... then you shall be a special treasure to Me above all people; for all the earth is Mine. And you shall be to Me a kingdom of priests and a holy nation' (Exodus 19:5,6). But rarely, throughout the long history of their nation, had they reached the standard of holiness God required of them. God's patience was remarkable and some 750 years later He is still pleading and reasoning with them through His prophet Isaiah.

ONE HUNDRED AND THIRTY-ONE: PETER'S PREPARATION

The remarkable way in which God prepared His servant to 'open the door of faith' to the Gentiles makes stirring reading. Two men praying, one a Roman centurion in his home in Caesarea and the other the apostle Peter on a rooftop in Joppa. The great sheet which in his trance he saw let down from heaven contained all manner of animals which according to the law of Leviticus 11 were unclean for a Jew to eat. Peter had overlooked the fact that the Lord Jesus had made all meats clean (see Mark 7:19 RV) and when he was instructed to eat, his notorious reply was 'Not so, Lord!' (Acts 10:14).

He was soon to learn that those words can never be linked together when addressing the Lord. 'What God has cleansed you must not call common' was the Lord's reply, which left him greatly wondering. And he was still wondering when in the over-ruling of His sovereign Lord, 'At that very moment' as he later recounted to his fellow-apostles, Cornelius' three messengers arrived at the door of Simon the tanner's home. 'Then the Spirit told me to go with them doubting nothing' he said, and it seems as though it was only when he entered Cornelius' home and listened to the story of the angel's message to him, that all his prejudices were overcome, for his opening word to the assembled gathering was 'In truth I perceive that God shows no partiality (or is no respecter of persons RV). But in every nation whoever fears Him and works righteousness is accepted by Him' (Acts 10:34,35).

ONE HUNDRED AND THIRTY-TWO: SALVATION IS NOT OF WORKS

Cornelius was an outstanding man, described by the Spirit of God as devout and one who feared God. His faith in the living God expressed itself in his prayers and almsgivings. Had the gospel never reached him he would surely have qualified for eternal life on the basis of Romans 2:7. But he was not satisfied. In prayer he was asking for further direction.

That is evident from the angel's message, that when he sent for Simon Peter: 'He will tell you what you must do' (Acts 10:6). In the kindness of God the gospel did reach him and he stands on the page of Scripture as a most impressive illustration of the truth that salvation is ' not of works, lest anyone should boast' (Ephesians 2:9). He needed to hear words by which he and his household would be saved. And right there in his home Peter was God's chosen vessel to bring those words to him. An angel's lips might be used to bring evangelist and seeker together, but through the lips of a redeemed man the message must be spoken.

And it was spoken in a most wonderful demonstration of the Holy Spirit's power. 'These things we also speak, not in words which man's wisdom teaches but which the Holy Spirit teaches' (1 Corinthians 2:13). Peter's preaching centred around two main points, to both of which he and his fellow-apostles had been witnesses; firstly of the Lord's life and service, ' all things which He did', how He 'went about doing good and healing all who were oppressed by the devil' (Acts 10:38); and secondly, how He was 'killed by hanging on a tree' and then manifested in resurrection life to witnesses 'who ate and drank with Him after He arose from the dead'. The twin facts of the death and resurrection of the Lord Jesus were prominent in all apostolic preaching, always leading up to the glorious truth that 'He is Lord of all' (Acts 10:34-43). 'God has made this Jesus, whom you crucified, both Lord and Christ' (Acts 2:36).

ONE HUNDRED AND THIRTY-THREE: MULTIPLYING BREAD

There was a famine in the land when Elisha came to Gilgal to meet the sons of the prophets. But there was a man from Baal Shalisha who had done some reaping despite the famine and he brought to Elisha the firstfruits of his harvest, twenty barley loaves and some newly ripened grain. Normally he would have taken it to God's house, but the ten tribes were not encouraged to go to Jerusalem, so he did the next best thing and brought it to God's prophet. Elisha told his servant to use it to feed the people. There were a hundred men in the place and the servant protested at the impossibility of feeding so many with so little. But he had not reckoned on the power of God, of course. Elisha simply repeated the instruction, 'Give it to the people, that they may eat' and then he added, ' for thus says the LORD: "They shall eat and have some left over."' It was a word from God and no word of His is void of power (2 Kings 4:42- 44).

God multiplied the loaves according to His promise, they were all fed and there was some left over. And so there was on the day the Lord Jesus fed five thousand men with five loaves and two fishes; and also when four thousand were fed with seven loaves and a few fishes. In both cases, it was a question of hungry multitudes and unbelieving disciples. 'Send the multitudes away' the disciples said. 'They do not need to go away' the Master replied. 'You give them something to eat.' And when they brought their few loaves and fishes and placed them in the Master's hands, He multiplied them to satisfy the need of every hungry person there. Not one of them went away unsatisfied. And He did it through the disciples. That precious and important point we must notice carefully (Matthew 14:15–21). It has been said so often before, but we must say it again, as long as there are spiritually hungry multitudes around us, as long as men and women, boys and girls who touch our lives are dying without having eaten of the bread of life. The food passed from His hands to the disciples' hands, so it actually came true, they did give them to eat.

They gathered up baskets full of broken pieces when the meal was over. There was enough and to spare. There always is in our heavenly Father's bountiful supply, but how shall His rich supply reach the hungry hearts of those around us unless we learn this vital lesson and are willing to put our little into His almighty hands? With His blessing, there is no limit to what the Lord can do with the little we are willing to put into His hands.

ONE HUNDRED AND THIRTY-FOUR: THE AXE-HEAD RAISED

Above the mantelpiece in a tiny home where an old missionary lady was spending her closing days, there was a wooden text with the words 'the iron did swim'. 'Did you ever see iron swimming?' she asked, with a twinkle in her eye. It was obvious she reckoned she had, and she went on to recount some of her experiences when the Lord had stepped in and done things which seemed to be impossible. The quotation comes from the story of Elisha, when at the request of the sons of the prophets he had accompanied them to Jordan to build a larger place for them to live in. As one of them worked away at cutting the wood his axe-head fell into the water, and he cried out in his distress, 'Alas, master! For it was borrowed.' Elisha's response was to ask exactly where it fell and, cutting a stick, he threw it into the water at that spot, and the Bible record says, 'he made the iron float', or as the Authorised Version says, 'the iron did swim' (2 Kings 6:6).

Only God could make that happen, of course. Humanly speaking, it was impossible. But is it not true that sometimes God intervenes in our lives doing seemingly impossible things in order to demonstrate His power and encourage our faith? God loves to stimulate our faith. 'Is anything too hard for the LORD?' was the question He put to Abraham when He promised him and Sarah a son in their old age (Genesis 18:14). It was left to Jeremiah to provide the plain answer to that question when he said, 'There is nothing too hard for You' (Jeremiah 32:17). Through deep experiences in life Jeremiah had watched the Lord doing wonderful things, delivering him in times of great danger and his faith had been strengthened as a result. And ours will be also. God may put our faith to the test at times and, as we learn to trust Him, we shall be strengthened for the next experience (1 Peter 1:7).

ONE HUNDRED AND THIRTY-FIVE: THE UNSEEN HOSTS

There is a spiritual world around us of which some are more conscious than others. The Bible says 'the things which are seen are temporary, but the things which are not seen are eternal' (2 Corinthians 4:18). However, the unseen, eternal things are every bit as real as the things we can see and handle. And they are infinitely more valuable, by as much as eternity is longer than time! We need to often remind ourselves of this fact and to be particularly mindful of the exhortation to 'seek those things which are above, where Christ is, sitting at the right hand of God. Set your mind on things above, not on things on the earth' (Colossians 3:1,2).

We are reminded of this by an incident in Elisha's life (2 Kings 6:8–23). He had been advising the king of Israel where the opposing king of Syria was planning to strike. When the king of Syria found out how the secret information was reaching Israel's king he sent his horsemen and chariots to take Elisha captive. One morning when Elisha's servant looked out he found the city surrounded by the Syrian hosts. 'Alas, my master! What shall we do?' he cried. Elisha's reply deserves our careful thought. 'Do not fear, for those who are with us are more than those who are with them' he said.

But the young man could not see anyone with them. They seemed to be all alone and that was why he was so alarmed. Elisha could see what he couldn't see, for the spiritual world around him was real to God's servant. He had seen the angels escorting Elijah to heaven as in a whirlwind and he had never forgotten it. He was conscious of the presence of those same angels right now when his life was in danger, and he simply asked the Lord to open the young man's eyes. And God did just that. He caused the servant to see what Elisha had been aware of all the time, a host of horses and chariots of fire, doubtless angelic beings, for Habakkuk wrote of the LORD riding upon His horses and His chariots of salvation (see 3:8). They formed a wall of protection around God's prophet and His servant.

The spiritual world is real. We know that. There are spiritual hosts of wickedness under the control of Satan, which are against us. But thank God there are also spiritual hosts under His control which are for us, and Elisha's word remains for ever true, 'those who are with us are more than those who are with them' (2 Kings 6:16). So, with the apostle Paul we say with confidence 'If God is for us, who can be against us?' We need the eyes of our hearts enlightened, do we not, so that we shall be more aware of our angel guardians, for 'Are they not all ministering spirits sent forth to minister for those who will inherit salvation?' (Hebrews 1:14).

ONE HUNDRED AND THIRTY-SIX: BOW AND ARROWS

Joash king of Israel reigned for sixteen years, but they were not good years, for he followed the evil ways of his predecessors. Toward the end of his life an interesting incident happened, for he came to bid farewell to Elisha who was terminally ill (see 2 Kings 13:14-20). He had probably ignored him during his lifetime, but now that the old prophet was about to depart, the king acknowledged the influence of his godly life. He used the same expression as Elisha used of Elijah when he was departing. He said, 'O my father, my father, the chariots of Israel and their horsemen!' How true that a nation's strength lies in its men of God, the men who speak God's word. Elijah's faith and prayers and messages from God had done more for Israel than the horsemen and chariots of her army. And so had Elisha's. Joash the king appeared to recognize that fact, despite all his failings.

Then the old prophet asked him to do an unusual thing. 'Take a bow and some arrows' he said, and then, 'Put your hand on the bow'. As he did so, Elisha put his hands over the king's hands. Do you get the picture: the old prophet standing beside the king as he opened the window toward the east, and together they directed the arrow and sent it toward its mark? 'The arrow of the LORD'S deliverance' declared Elisha, to remind the king that any victory gained over the enemy would be by the Lord's help and strength and not his own. As with Joseph before him, his hands would be 'made strong by the hands of the Mighty God of Jacob' (Genesis 49:24). That was the lesson Elisha wanted to convey to the king and it was his last message before he died.

What an important lesson it was, not only for the king, but for us, too, for it applies for all time. Any victory achieved in our lives of service for the Lord will be by the strength that He supplies. 'I can do all things through Christ who strengthens me', was the apostle Paul's testimony (Philippians 4:13). And more than that, he found that his very weakness was the opportunity for the Lord to demonstrate His power. So he learned to take pleasure in anything which cast him in dependence upon the Lord, for 'when I am weak, then I am strong', he said (2 Corinthians 12:10).

ONE HUNDRED AND THIRTY-SEVEN: A CRY FROM THE CROSS

Psalm 22 is clearly recognized as a psalm of the cross. Eleven times the gospel writers either quote directly from it or refer to statements in it. His physical suffering at the hands of cruel men is plainly foretold; the excruciating pain through suspension on a cross by pierced hands and feet, bones wrenched out of joint, thirst so intense that His tongue cleaved to His jaws. It is all there in the psalm including the mental anguish as priests and elders hurled their cruel jibes at Him, shooting out their lips and shaking their heads in derision as they mocked His trust in God.

It is remarkable how much of David's own experience is used by the Holy Spirit to reveal the intensity of the Lord's sufferings. But the psalm takes us beyond David's experience to suffering which could only have been true of the Lord Jesus. It seems as though His holy mind was going over the words of this very psalm as He hung upon the tree. David was one of the nation's fathers who were never forsaken when they called on God in times of distress. 'But I am a worm, and no man' He cried, 'A reproach of men, and despised of the people'. 'My God, My God, why have You forsaken Me?' As another of our poets has movingly expressed it: "Out from the darkness rings an awful cry, The lonely, orphan cry of suffering love, That reached the very heart of God on high, Yet brought no answer from the Throne above" (Albert G. Jarvis). Did His cry really reach His Father's heart? We believe it did, for 'God was in Christ' the scripture says, 'reconciling the world to Himself' (2 Corinthians 5:19).

ONE HUNDRED AND THIRTY-EIGHT: THE JEALOUSY OF MIRIAM AND AARON

The word 'jealousy' is not mentioned in Numbers 12 where this sad incident is recorded, but plainly it was the underlying cause of the dispute, family jealousy, and it must have been very hard on Moses. Evidently Miriam was the instigator, for she bore the punishment. Miriam his big sister, whom he so dearly loved, who had watched over him when as a babe he lay in his bulrush ark by the river bank, had gained Aaron's ear and together they spoke against their brother. The occasion of their complaint had to do with the woman whom he had married.

If it seems strange that their disapproval of Moses' wife should have been raised after so many years of marriage, it may serve to underline the fact that their complaint was a cover for a deeper grievance that had grown into jealousy of his position and his nearness to the Lord. 'Has the LORD indeed spoken only through Moses? Has He not spoken through us also?' they asked. And scripture records the ominous words 'And the LORD heard it'. Of course He did. Does He not hear all we say? And does not that fact emphasize the importance of James' plain instruction, 'Do not speak evil of one another, brethren' (4:11)? That is clear and unambiguous. Don't do it!

How did Moses cope? In an exemplary way, which we do well to note carefully against the time when we might find ourselves in similar circumstance. And the secret of his ability to do so lies in the third verse of the chapter: 'the man Moses was very humble, more than all men who were on the face of the earth'. Meek is the word used in the Authorised Version and Revised Version and humility and meekness are closely linked, although not entirely the same. Humility produces meekness. The one follows the other in Colossians 3:12 as two of the qualities we are to put on as God's elect.

MORE BOOKS FROM ALAN TOMS

WHERE IS GOD'S HOUS TODAY?

Is God is dwelling among men on earth today? Where is His dwelling place? How may I be sure of a place in it? This book was written because believers want to know the answers to these important questions. It looks firstly at the Old Testament – remembering that 'whatsoever things were written before were written for our learning' (Romans 15:4) and that the tabernacle which Moses built is said in the New Testament to be a symbol or parable for the present time (Hebrews 9:9). As these lessons are applied to what is written in the New Testament, the author's prayer is that God's Holy Spirit will make clear the lessons He wants believers to learn in regard to the worship and service of God today.

ETERNAL SECURITY

One of the concerns and doubts that can plague a Christian is that, although he has been saved by the work of Christ, if he falls back into the world and loses his love for the Lord, he will be eternally lost. That is, he may be saved one day and lost the next'. If this were true, it would surely be better for him to be ushered into eternity while he is still in the state of being saved. But is it true? Can that belief be supported from the Scriptures? That is the question that Alan seeks to answer in this book.

1. The Good Shepherd And His Sheep
2. Eternal Life As A Gift
3. The Judgement Seat Of Christ

4. Shall We Continue In Sin?

5. Children Of God

6. Daily Defilement

7. Fruitbearing

8. Falling Away

9. The Indwelling Holy Spirit

10. Salvation In Three Aspects

11. Summary Of Main Points

ALIVE UNTO GOD

The author was approached at an evening campfire at a Bible camp by a group of young people who had a number of important questions about relationships, sex and holy living – the discussion went long into the night as the Bible's answers were applied to each question. Out of that discussion came this little book.

ABOUT HAYES PRESS

Hayes Press (www.hayespress.org) is a registered charity in the United Kingdom, whose primary mission is to disseminate the Word of God, mainly through literature. It is one of the largest distributors of gospel tracts and leaflets in the United Kingdom, with over 100 titles and many thousands dispatched annually. In addition to paperbacks and eBooks, Hayes Press also publishes Plus Eagles' Wings, a fun and educational Bible magazine for children, and Golden Bells, a popular daily Bible reading calendar in wall or desk formats.

If you would like to contact Hayes Press, there are a number of ways you can do so:

By mail: c/o The Barn, Flaxlands, Royal Wootton Bassett, Wiltshire, UK SN4 8DY

By phone: 01793 850598

By eMail:info@hayespress.org

via Facebook: www.facebook.com/hayespress.org

www.ingramcontent.com/pod-product-compliance
Lightning Source LLC
Chambersburg PA
CBHW071339150726
47997CB00002B/793